Vegan Comfort Foods Cookbook

Table Of Contents

Macaroni-and-'Cheese' Casserole 6

Mashed Potatoes with Roasted Garlic 7

Blueberry Pancakes 8

Vegetable Lasagna 9

Creamy Vegan Zucchini Casserole 10

Avocado Cream Pasta 11

Apple Muffins with Cinnamon 12

Vegan Shepherd's Pie 13

Moroccan Spiced Cauliflower and Almond Soup 15

Tofu Popcorn Chick'n 16

Cauliflower Hot Wings 17

Falafel Burgers 18

Minty Pea and Potato Soup 19

Chickpea, Tomato and Spinach Curry 20

Vegan Garlic Buffalo Brussels Sprouts 22

Spring Rolls with Carrot-Ginger Dipping Sauce 24

Corn Potato Chowder 26

Spicy Carrot Soup 27

Hummus Pizza with Veggies 28

Mushroom Creamy Soup 30

Tofu Peanut Satay and Cucumber Skewerst 31

Cauliflower Leek Casserole 33

Eggplant Steaks with Tomato Salad 34

Cheesy Mexican Tortilla Bake 35

Tomato Basil Soup 36

Vegan Club Sandwich 37

Creamy Red Pepper Alfredo Pasta 38

Sesame Noodles 39

Vegan Pot Pie 40

Vegan Spaghetti alla Puttanesca	42
Grits with Tempeh Sausage and Brussels Sprouts	44
Minestrone Soup	46
Mushrooms and Peas Vegan Risotto	47
Stewed Chickpeas and Chard Toast	49
Broccoli Quinoa Gratin	50
Vegan Spinach Artichoke Quesadillas	52
Quinoa and Roasted Pepper Chili	53
Ratatouille	54
Vegan Meatballs	55
Creamed Spinach	56
Vegan Burrito	57
Tacos	58
Pepperoni Pizza	59
Spinach Artichoke Pizza	60
Mushroom Bean Burger	61
Vegan Jambalaya	62
Creamy Lemon Pepper Chickpeas	63
Potato Pancakes	64
Tofu and Cauliflower Balti	65
Coconut Apple Ginger Dal	67
Vegetable Risotto	68
Coconut Curry Ramen	70
Sweet Potato Noodle Pasta	72
Vegan Poutine	74
Cauliflower Rice Kitchari	76
Moroccan-Spiced Eggplant and Tomato Stew	78
Red Curry with Roasted Vegetables	80
Vegan Pizza	82
Vegan Thai Curry	84

Lentil Lasagna 86

Mushroom Stroganoff 88

Chipotle Tofu Chilaquiles 90

Mushroom Bolognese 91

Broccoli Leek Casserole 93

Pumpkin Pasta with Spinach and Mushrooms 95

Fettuccine Cauliflower Alfredo 97

Zucchini Casserole 98

Roasted Red Pepper Pasta with Black Pepper Chickpeas 99

Mexican Lasagna 101

Creamy Broccoli Cheese Soup 103

Grilled Cheese with Smoky Tomato Soup 105

French Dip Sandwiches 107

French Toast 109

Chickpea Flour Omelette 110

Tofu Benedict with Avocado 112

Pumpkin Chili 114

Vegan Meatloaf 115

Baked Squash 117

Caesar Salad 119

Vegan Cobb Salad 120

Veggie Dogs 121

Eggplant Parmesan with Cashew Ricotta 123

Lasagna with Basil Cashew Cheese 125

Lentil Steaks with Mushroom Gravy 127

Vegan Carbonara 129

Vegan Tortilla Soup 130

Mushroom Bean Avocado Toast 132

Roasted Cauliflowers with Tomato Sauce 133

Tofu Cashew Coconut Curry 134

Vegan Frittata	135
Spinach Ravioli	136
Peanut Noodles	137
Creamy Vegan Pasta	138
Taco Pizza	139
Vegan Chili Cheese Fries	141
Saucy Meatballs with Spaghetti	143
Chickpea Curry with Potatoes	145
Classic Vegan Coleslaw	146
Herbed Potato, Asparagus and Chickpeas	147
Banana Chia Pudding	149

Macaroni-and-'Cheese' Casserole

Cooking time: 20 minutes   **Servings**: 4-6

Ingredients:

- 3 ½ cups elbow macaroni
- 4 cups water
- 3 ½ cup boiling water
- ½ cup vegan margarine
- ½ cup flour
- 2 tablespoons soy sauce
- 1 ½ teaspoon garlic powder
- ½ teaspoon paprika
- ¼ cup vegetable oil
- 1 cup nutritional yeast
- A pinch of turmeric
- Salt, to taste

Instructions:

1. Preheat the oven to 350F.
2. Bring water to a boil in a medium sauce pan. Cook macaroni as per package instructions. Drain.
3. Preheat margarine in a pan over low heat until melted. Add flour, whisk well to combine.
4. Continue cooking until smooth, stirring constantly.
5. Add 3 ½ cup boiling water, soy sauce, garlic powder, paprika, turmeric and salt. Stir until combined.
6. Add oil and nutritional yeast. Add pasta and toss well to coat. Transfer to a casserole dish.
7. Bake for 15 minutes and then broil for 1-2 minutes until crisp.

Nutritional info (per serving): 289 calories; 7 g fat; 45 g carbohydrate; 10 g protein

Mashed Potatoes with Roasted Garlic

Cooking time: 35 minutes   **Servings**: 4

Ingredients:

- 4 potatoes, peeled and quartered
- 1 garlic head
- 1 teaspoon olive oil
- 4 tablespoons vegan butter
- ½ cup soy milk
- Fresh chives
- Salt, pepper, to taste

Instructions:

1. Preheat the oven to 430F.
2. Peel the outer layer of garlic head, chop off the tips of the garlic. Wrap in foil and drizzle with olive oil. Close the foil and bake for 35 minutes.
3. Add potatoes to the pot and cover with water. Bring to a boil and cook for 20-25 minutes.
4. Drain water let rest for 2-3 minutes.
5. Add vegan butter and mash potatoes with a masher.
6. Add soy milk, ¼ cup at a time and mashing it in, until smooth.
7. Pop the cloves of the garlic out, mash with a fork. Add to potatoes.
8. Add salt and black pepper to taste. Serve topped with fresh chives.

Nutritional info (per serving): 333 calories; 9.2 g fat; 56 g carbohydrate; 6.6 g protein

Blueberry Pancakes

Cooking time: 30 minutes

Servings: 15-20

Ingredients:

- 2 cups flour
- 3 tablespoons sugar
- 1 tablespoon baking powder
- 3 tablespoons coconut oil
- 2 cups soy or almond milk
- ½ cup fresh or frozen blueberries
- ½ teaspoon salt

Instructions:

1. Mix flour, sugar, baking powder and salt in a bowl.
2. Add milk and oil and mix well until combined. Add blueberries and stir to combine.
3. Preheat a non stick pan over medium heat, pour about 1-2 tablespoons of batter to a skillet. Cook for about 3 minutes per side.
4. Serve topped with syrup or fruits.

Nutritional info (per serving): 159 calories; 3 g fat; 30 g carbohydrate; 4 g protein

Vegetable Lasagna

Cooking time: 1 hour   **Servings**: 8

Ingredients:

- 1 box lasagna noodles
- 4 ½ cups jarred marinara
- 1 cup cashew ricotta
- 1 ½ cups fresh spinach
- 2 ½ cups mixed vegetables, chopped, fresh
- ½ cup vegan parmesan cheese

Instructions:

1. Preheat the oven to 375F. Mix spinach and ricotta in a bowl.
2. Spread about 2 cups sauce on the bottom of a baking dish.
3. Add raw lasagna noodles, top with more sauce.
4. Add veggies on top and more lasagna noodles. Sprinkle with half of Parmesan. Top with the remaining noodles.
5. Top with the remaining sauce. Add the remaining Parmesan on top.
6. Cover with foil and bake for 45 minutes. Remove foil and bake for 15 minutes more. Let cool before serving.

Nutritional info (per serving): 433 calories; 9 g fat; 32 g carbohydrate; 14 g protein

Creamy Vegan Zucchini Casserole

Cooking time: 30 minutes   **Servings**: 4-6

Ingredients:

- 3 zucchini, sliced
- 2 cups cherry tomatoes, halved
- 1 cup creamy vegan cheese
- ¼ cup fresh basil, chopped
- 4 garlic cloves, crushed
- 2 tablespoons olive oil
- ¼ teaspoon smoked paprika
- 1 pinch cayenne pepper
- Salt, pepper, to taste

Instructions:

1. Preheat the oven to 375F. Mix zucchini, garlic, basil, olive oil, smoked paprika, salt and pepper in a bowl. Mix well to coat zucchini.
2. Spread zucchini mixture on the bottom of a baking dish.
3. Spread vegan cheese on top of zucchini layer. Repeat layers until all the ingredients are used. Top with the cherry tomatoes and the final layer of cheese.
4. Season with cayenne pepper. Bake for about 30 minutes.

Nutritional info (per serving): 293 calories; 24.2 g fat; 14.7 g carbohydrate; 6.7 g protein

Avocado Cream Pasta

Cooking time: 30 minutes **Servings**: 4-6

Ingredients:

- 2 avocados, pitted and diced
- 2 cups pasta of choice, cooked
- 1 garlic clove, minced
- ½ lemon, juiced
- ¼ cup unsweetened soy milk
- ¼ cup water
- 4 cherry tomatoes, halved
- Salt, to taste
- A pinch of red pepper flakes

Instructions:

1. Add avocado, garlic and lemon juice to a food processor or a blender. Process until smooth.
2. Add soy milk and water. Add salt and red pepper. Process until combined.
3. Pour sauce over pasta and toss well to coat, serve.

Nutritional info (per serving): 639 calories; 33 g fat; 77 g carbohydrate; 14 g protein

Apple Muffins with Cinnamon

Cooking time: 25 minutes **Servings**: 12

Ingredients:

- 1 tablespoon ground flax
- 3 tablespoons water
- 3 cups whole wheat flour
- 2 teaspoons baking powder
- ½ cup sugar
- A pinch salt
- 2 teaspoons vanilla extract
- 1 cup non-dairy milk
- ½ cup lemon juice
- ½ cup unsweetened apple juice
- ½ cup apples, peeled, chopped
- 1 ½ teaspoons ground cinnamon
- 3 tablespoons coconut oil
- 3 tablespoons rolled oats
- 3 tablespoons walnuts, chopped

Instructions:

1. Preheat the oven to 400F. Prepare the muffin tins and grease with cooking spray.
2. Mix cinnamon, oil, rolled oats and walnuts in a bowl. Set aside.
3. Mix ground flax and water in a separate bowl. Add flour, baking powder, sugar and salt, mix well to combine.
4. Mix vanilla, milk, apple juice and lemon juice in a bowl. Add dry mixture to the wet mixture and stir well to combine.
5. Pour the batter into muffin tins, top with cinnamon mixture. Bake for 25 minutes. Let cool before serving.

Nutritional info (per serving): 155 calories; 4.9 g fat; 26.8 g carbohydrate; 1.5 g protein

Vegan Shepherd's Pie

Cooking time: 1 hour 20 minutes   **Servings**: 8

Ingredients:

- 2 ½ lbs King Edward potatoes
- 2 tablespoons vegetable oil
- 2 tablespoons dried porcini mushrooms, soaked in hot water for 15 mins, drained
- 2 leeks, chopped
- 2 onions, chopped
- 4 celery ribs, chopped
- 14 oz canned chickpeas
- 8 oz frozen peas
- 8 oz fresh spinach
- 1 butternut squash, peeled and cut into cubes
- 2 tablespoons tomato purée
- 4 carrots, cut into cubes
- 1 vegetable stock cube
- 3 garlic cloves, crushed
- 2 teaspoons smoked paprika
- 1 tablespoon fresh oregano, chopped
- ½ teaspoon thyme
- 1 teaspoon sage leaves, chopped
- 2 tablespoons olive oil
- Salt, pepper, to taste

Instructions:

1. Add potatoes (unpeeled) to a sauce pan and cover with water. Bring to a boil and cook for 40 minutes. Drain and let cool.
2. Preheat vegetable oil in a pan and add mushrooms, leeks, onions, carrots and stock cube, cook for 5 minutes. Stir occasionally.

3. Add garlic, tomato purée, paprika, squash, oregano, thyme and sage. Stir well and cook for 3 minutes. Add celery and cook for 2 minutes more.
4. Add chickpeas with canned water, spinach and stir well. Cook for 5 minutes, season with salt and pepper.
5. Peel the potatoes and mash with a fork. Add about 1 cup of potatoes to vegetables, mix the rest with olive oil and season with salt and pepper.
6. Transfer everything to a pie pan and top with mashed potatoes. Preheat the oven to 375F. Bake for 40-45 minutes. Serve with vegan tomato ketchup.

Nutritional info (per serving): 396 calories; 5.3 g fat; 72 g carbohydrate; 17.7 g protein

Moroccan Spiced Cauliflower and Almond Soup

Cooking time: 25 minutes   **Servings**: 4

Ingredients:

- 1 large cauliflower head, cut into small florets
- 2 tablespoons olive oil
- 2 tablespoons harissa paste
- ½ teaspoon cinnamon
- ½ teaspoon cumin
- ½ teaspoon coriander
- 4 cups hot vegetable stock
- 2 tablespoons toasted flaked almond

Instructions:

1. Preheat oil in a non stick pan. Add cinnamon, coriander and cumin, stir once and add paste. Cook for 2 minutes.
2. Add cauliflower florets, almonds and stock. Cover the pan and cook for 20 minutes.
3. Let cool a little. Transfer soup to a blender and process until smooth. Serve topped with almonds.

Nutritional info (per serving): 116 calories; 8 g fat; 9 g carbohydrate; 4 g protein

Tofu Popcorn Chick'n

Cooking time: 15 minutes **Servings**: 8

Ingredients:

- 13 oz extra firm tofu
- ⅓ cup chickpea flour
- ¼ cup nutritional yeast
- 1 tablespoon mustard
- 1 teaspoon Cajun seasoning
- 1 teaspoon salt
- ½ teaspoon pepper
- ½ cup water
- 3 tablespoons extra virgin olive oil

Instructions:

1. Put something heavy on top of tofu, press for 10 minutes. Drain and set aside.
2. Mix flour, nutritional yeast, Cajun seasoning, salt and pepper in a bowl.
3. Add water slowly and whisk well until combined.
4. Add mustard and mix well. Break tofu into big chunks. Add to the flour mixture and toss well to coat.
5. Preheat oil in a non stick pan. Add tofu mixture to the pan and cook on all sides until golden. Serve.

Nutritional info (per serving): 132 calories; 8.4 g fat; 8.7 g carbohydrate; 8.1g protein

Cauliflower Hot Wings

Cooking time: 50 minutes **Servings**: 4

Ingredients:

- 1 cauliflower head, broken into florets
- ¾ cup flour
- ¾ cup almond milk, unsweetened
- ¼ cup water
- ¾ cup breadcrumbs
- 1 cup spicy BBQ sauce
- 2 teaspoons garlic powder
- 1 ½ teaspoons paprika
- 1 teaspoon Sriracha sauce
- 2 green onions, sliced
- Salt, pepper, to taste

Instructions:

1. Preheat the oven to 350F. Line a baking sheet with parchment paper.
2. Mix flour, milk, water, garlic power, paprika, salt, and black pepper in a bowl.
3. Dip the cauliflower florets into the flour milk mixture, coat well.
4. Dip them into panko breadcrumbs.
5. Lay the cauliflower florets on the baking sheet in one layer. Bake for 25 minutes.
6. Transfer the cooked cauliflower wings to a bowl. Mix BBQ sauce and sriracha sauce, pour it over the cauliflower wings. Coat them from all sides.
7. Put the coated hot wings back on the baking sheet and bake again for 20 minutes.
8. Serve topped with green onions. Enjoy!

Nutritional info (per serving): 388 calories; 12.4 g fat; 63.1 g carbohydrate; 8 g protein

Falafel Burgers

Cooking time: 6 minutes   **Servings**: 4

Ingredients:

- 1 can (14 oz) chickpeas, rinsed and drained
- 1 red onion, chopped
- 1 garlic clove, chopped
- 1 teaspoon ground cumin
- 1 teaspoon ground coriander
- ½ teaspoon chilli powder
- 2 tablespoons flour
- 2 tablespoons sunflower oil
- 7 oz tomato salsa
- Green salad, for serving
- Pita bread, toasted, for serving
- A handful parsley

Instructions:

1. Add chickpeas, onion, garlic, parsley, cumin, coriander, chilli powder and flour to a food processor. Blend until smooth.
2. Form medium sized patties out of the mixture. Preheat oil in a frying pan over medium heat.
3. Add patties and cook for about 3 minutes on each side.
4. Serve on toasted pita bread, with tomato salsa and salad.

Nutritional info (per serving): 161 calories; 8 g fat; 18 g carbohydrate; 6 g protein

Minty Pea and Potato Soup

Cooking time: 25 minutes   **Servings**: 4

Ingredients:

- 2 lbs potatoes, peeled, cubed
- 1 onion, chopped
- 2 teaspoons vegetable oil
- 4 cups vegetable stock
- 1 ½ cups frozen peas
- A handful fresh mint, chopped
- Salt, pepper, to taste

Instructions:

1. Preheat oil in a large saucepan over medium heat. Add onion and cook for about 4-5 minutes until soft.
2. Add potatoes and stock, bring to the boil. Cover the pan and simmer for 10-15 minutes.
3. In the last 2 minutes of cooking add peas.
4. Let the soup cool a little, then transfer to a blender (or you can use immersion blender instead). Blend until smooth.
5. Season to taste and serve topped with mint.

Nutritional info (per serving): 249 calories; 3 g fat; 48 g carbohydrate; 11 g protein

Chickpea, Tomato and Spinach Curry

Cooking time: 40 minutes   **Servings**: 6

Ingredients:

- 1 onion, chopped
- 6 tomatoes
- 1 broccoli head, broken into small florets
- 1 can (14 oz) chickpeas, drained
- ½ cup baby spinach leaves
- 2 garlic cloves, chopped
- 1 ¼ inch piece ginger, grated
- ½ tablespoon oil

- 1 teaspoon ground cumin
- 2 teaspoons ground coriander
- 1 teaspoon turmeric
- 1 teaspoon yeast
- 4 tablespoons red lentils
- 6 tablespoons coconut cream
- 1 lemon, juiced
- 1 tablespoon toasted sesame seeds
- 1 tablespoon chopped cashew

Instructions:

1. Add onion, garlic, ginger and tomatoes to a blender or a food processor. Blend until pureed.
2. Preheat oil in a pan over medium heat. Add all the spices and cook for 1 minute, add puree and yeast. Cook for about 2 minutes until bubbly.

3. Add lentils and coconut cream, cook until lentils are soft. Add broccoli and cook for 4 minutes more.
4. Add chickpeas and spinach, add lemon juice, sesame seeds and cashew. Stir well to combine. Serve over rice.

Nutritional info (per serving): 204 calories; 7 g fat; 20 g carbohydrate; 11 g protein

Vegan Garlic Buffalo Brussels Sprouts

Cooking time: 35 minutes **Servings:** 6

Ingredients:

- 16 oz Brussels sprouts, ends trimmed
- 3 cups Panko bread crumbs
- 1 cup almond milk
- 1 teaspoon apple cider vinegar
- ¾ cup all purpose flour
- ½ cup corn starch
- 2 teaspoon hot sauce
- ½ cup hot sauce
- ½ cup vegan butter
- 1 tablespoon agave syrup
- 1 teaspoon soy sauce
- 8 garlic cloves, chopped
- Salt, to taste

Instructions:

1. Preheat the oven to 425F.
2. Mix almond milk and apple cider vinegar in a bowl. Let rest for about a minute.
3. Mix flour, cornstarch and salt in a separate bowl. Whisk 2 teaspoons of hot sauce to the almond milk mixture, pour the mixture on top of flour mixture and stir well. Whisk until fully combined.

4. Dip each Brussels sprout first in batter and then in Panko breadcrumbs. Spread on a sheet pan layered with parchment paper.
5. Bake for 10 minutes, flip each sprout and bake for another 10-15 minutes.
6. Meanwhile, cook the sauce. Preheat began butter in a skillet over medium heat. Add garlic and cook for 2 minutes. Add hot sauce, agave, say sauce. Cook for 1 minute more.
7. Serve cooked sprouts with the sauce.

Nutritional info (per serving): 406 calories; 12.8 g fat; 64.9 g carbohydrate; 11.2 g protein

Spring Rolls with Carrot-Ginger Dipping Sauce

Cooking time: 55 minutes   **Servings:** 6

Ingredients:

- 6 rice-paper wrappers
- 2 cups radish sprouts (1/2 ounce)
- 1 red beet, trimmed and thinly sliced crosswise
- 1 medium carrot, peeled and julienned
- 1 cucumber, julienned
- 1 red bell pepper, stem and seeds removed, julienned
- 3/4 cup coarsely grated daikon
- 3 medium carrots, peeled and coarsely chopped
- 1 small shallot, quartered
- 2 tablespoons coarsely grated peeled fresh ginger
- 1/4 cup rice-wine vinegar (not seasoned)
- 2 tablespoons low-sodium soy sauce
- 1/4 teaspoon toasted sesame oil
- salt and freshly ground pepper, to taste
- 1/4 cup vegetable oil
- 1/4 cup water

Instructions:

To make the spring rolls:
1. Soak one rice-paper wrapper in a large bowl of hot water until pliable. Transfer to a work surface.
2. Place one-sixth of the sprouts, beet slices, carrot, cucumber, bell pepper, and daikon on the wrapper, towards the bottom. Fold ends in and roll tightly to enclose filling.
3. Repeat with remaining ingredients to make 5 more rolls.
4. To make the dipping sauce:

5. Puree carrots, shallot, ginger, vinegar, soy sauce, sesame oil, salt, and pepper in a food processor until smooth.
6. With machine running, add vegetable oil and then water through the feed tube in a slow, steady stream.
7. Serve sauce with spring rolls.

Nutritional info (per serving): 120 calories; 9.4 g fat; 9 g carbohydrate; 1.5 g protein

Corn Potato Chowder

Cooking time: 20 minutes   **Servings:** 4

Ingredients:

- 4 medium or large potatoes, peeled and diced
- 2 carrots, chopped
- 1 onion, chopped
- 2 stalks celery, chopped
- 2 garlic cloves, minced
- 3 cups water or vegetable broth
- 3 cups almond or soy milk
- 1 cup fresh or frozen corn kernels
- 1 tablespoon olive oil
- ¼ cup flour
- 3 tablespoons nutritional yeast
- ½ teaspoon dried oregano
- ½ teaspoon dried thyme
- Salt, pepper, to taste

Instructions:

1. Preheat oil in a big pot over medium heat. Add onions and cook for 2 minutes. Add garlic, carrots and celery, sauté for 4-5 minutes.
2. Add flour, oregano and thyme, mix well. Sauté for couple of minutes to coat the vegetables with flour, until flour starts turning brown.
3. Add potatoes, broth, milk and nutritional yeast, mix well. Bring soup to a boil and cook over medium heat for about 10 minutes until potatoes are soft.
4. After that add corn, salt and pepper to taste and cook for 2 more minutes. Turn off the heat and serve!

Nutritional info (per serving): 176 calories; 3 g fat; 31 g carbohydrate; 5 g protein

Spicy Carrot Soup

Cooking time: 40 minutes   **Servings:** 4

Ingredients:

- 10-12 big carrots, peeled and chopped
- 1 onion, chopped
- 2 garlic cloves, crushed
- 1 tablespoon coconut oil
- 1 can (14 oz) coconut milk
- 3 teaspoons red curry paste
- 4 cups vegetable stock or water
- 1/3 cup peanut butter
- Salt, pepper, to taste

Instructions:

1. Heat coconut oil in a big pot over medium heat. Add onions and cook for 3 minutes until soften. Add red curry paste and garlic, cook for 1 more minutes stirring well.
2. Add stock or water, milk and carrots. Bring soup to a boil, reduce the heat to low and cook covered for 25-30 minutes.
3. Add peanut butter, salt and pepper, mix well. Use blender to puree the soup until smooth.
4. Add more salt and pepper if needed and serve.

Nutritional info (per serving): 238 calories; 7 g fat; 34 g carbohydrate; 11 g protein

Hummus Pizza with Veggies

Cooking time: 20 minutes **Servings:** 6-8

Ingredients:

- 3 ½ cups flour
- 8-10 mushrooms, sliced
- 1 cup hummus
- 1 teaspoon salt
- 1 teaspoon instant yeast
- 1 pinch sugar
- 3 tablespoons olive oil
- 1 cup warm water
- 1 handful fresh spinach
- ½ cup black olives
- ½ cup artichoke hearts in oil, chopped
- ½ cup cherry tomatoes, halved
- ½ red onion, sliced
- 2 teaspoons dried oregano
- Red pepper flakes, to taste

Instructions:

1. Mix flour, salt, yeast and sugar in a bowl. Add oil and water. Knead with your hands until smooth dough is formed.

2. Form into a ball and cover with plastic wrap. Let rest in a warm place for about an hour, until doubles in size.
3. Preheat the oven to 350F.
4. Transfer the dough to a working surface, dusted with flour. Divide into two balls and form into two pizzas.
5. Spread hummus on top of pizzas, add olives, spinach, artichoke, tomatoes and onion on top. Season with oregano and red pepper flakes. Bake for 20 minutes.

Nutritional info (per serving): 423 calories; 13.1 g fat; 65.2 g carbohydrate; 12.2 g protein

Mushroom Creamy Soup

Cooking time: 10 minutes　　　　　　**Servings:** 4

Ingredients:

- 2 lb mushrooms, sliced
- 1 onion, chopped
- 2 garlic cloves, chopped
- 5 cups almond milk or any other plant milk
- 3 cups vegetable stock
- 1 teaspoon ground ginger
- 1 teaspoon lemon juice
- 2 tablespoons fresh parsley, chopped
- Salt, pepper, to taste

Instructions:

1. Put mushrooms, onion and garlic into a big pot. Add vegetable stock and milk and bring soup to a boil over medium heat. Cook for 10 minutes.
2. Puree the soup with a blender. Add salt, pepper, ginger and lemon juice.
3. Serve soup topped with fresh parsley.

Nutritional info (per serving): 324 calories; 12 g fat; 44.2 g carbohydrate; 12 g protein

Tofu Peanut Satay and Cucumber Skewerst

Cooking time: 10-15 minutes   **Servings:** 4

Ingredients:

- 1 block firm tofu, cubed
- 1 English cucumber, peeled into long thin ribbons
- 1 tablespoon peanut butter + 3 tablespoons
- 3 tablespoons tamari sauce + 2 teaspoons
- 2 tablespoons sesame oil
- 2 tablespoons maple syrup + 2 teaspoons
- 2 garlic cloves, minced
- ¼ cup coconut milk
- 1 tablespoon lime juice
- 1 teaspoon ginger, minced
- 1 pinch red pepper flakes
- 1 pinch sea salt
- ½ cup toasted peanuts, chopped
- 1 cup fresh mint leaves, chopped

Instructions:

1. Preheat the grill to medium high.
2. Mix 1 tablespoon peanut butter, 3 tablespoons tamari sauce, 2 tablespoons sesame oil, 2 tablespoons maple syrup and 1 garlic clove in a bowl. Add tofu cubes and toss well to coat. Let marinate for 10-15 minutes.
3. Cook the satay sauce. Mix coconut milk, 3 tablespoons peanut butter, 1 tablespoon lime juice, 2 teaspoons tamari sauce, 2 teaspoons maple syrup, ginger, 1 garlic clove, sea salt and pepper flakes in a bowl. Stir until smooth.

4. Thread the marinated tofu onto skewers. Place the skewers on the grill and cook for 3-4 minutes per side.
5. Mix cucumber slices with the cooked sauce in a bowl. Top the skewers with chopped peanuts, sauce (satay) drizzle and mint leaves. Serve with cucumbers.

Nutritional info (per serving): 239 calories; 20.6 g fat; 9.74 g carbohydrate; 8.3 g protein

Cauliflower Leek Casserole

Cooking time: 40 minutes   **Servings:** 4-6

Ingredients:

- ½ cauliflower head, cut into florets
- 3 cups leeks, chopped
- 1 cup raw cashews, soaked for at least 4 hours
- 2 garlic cloves
- 2 cups water
- 2/3 cup nutritional yeast
- ¼ teaspoon paprika
- ¼ teaspoon cayenne pepper
- Fresh parsley, chopped
- Salt, black pepper, to taste

Instructions:

1. Preheat the oven to 390F.
2. Steam cauliflower florets in a steamer for 5 -7 minutes until tender. Toss cauliflower and leeks together, transfer to a casserole dish.
3. Add cashews, garlic, water, nutritional yeast, salt and pepper to a food processor or a blender. Process until smooth.
4. Pour sauce on top of cauliflower and leeks until well covered. Bake for 40 minutes until sauce has thickened and leeks have softened and wilted.
5. Remove casserole dish from oven. Sprinkle with paprika, cayenne pepper and chopped fresh parsley.

Nutritional info (per serving): 352 calories; 25.9 g fat; 14 g carbohydrate; 15.4 g protein

Eggplant Steaks with Tomato Salad

Cooking time: 30 minutes   **Servings:** 4

Ingredients:

- 2 eggplants, thickly sliced
- ¼ cup balsamic vinegar + 1 tablespoon
- 1 tablespoon oil
- 6 roma tomatoes, chopped
- 2 garlic cloves, chopped
- ½ red onion, chopped
- ¼ cup parsley, chopped
- Salt, pepper, to taste

Instructions:

1. Season eggplant slices with salt and let rest for 30 minutes. Wash and pat dry.
2. Mix balsamic vinegar (1/4 cup), salt and pepper in a bowl. Add eggplant steaks and coat well with the mixture.
3. Preheat the oven to 400F. Cover the baking sheet with parchment paper and place steaks on the sheet. Bake steaks for 20 minutes.
4. Meanwhile, mix tomatoes, garlic, onion, parsley and 1 tablespoon vinegar in a bowl. Add oil and toss well to coat.
5. Serve steaks topped with tomato salad.

Nutritional info (per serving): 363 calories; 13 g fat; 53 g carbohydrate; 12 g protein

Cheesy Mexican Tortilla Bake

Cooking time: 25 minutes

Servings: 4-6

Ingredients:

- 1 cup raw unsalted cashews
- 1 cup salsa
- ¾ cup plain dairy-free yogurt
- ¼ cup water
- 1 ¼ teaspoons smoked paprika
- 1 ¼ teaspoons ground cumin
- 1 teaspoon fine sea salt
- 9 small corn tortillas, quartered
- 2 cans (15 oz) low-sodium black beans, drained and rinsed
- 2 cups frozen sweet corn
- Green onions, for serving

Instructions:

1. Preheat the oven to 350 F. Add cashews, yogurt, paprika, water, cumin and salt to a blender and process until smooth.
2. Place the salsa on the bottom of the baking dish, in one layer. Top with tortillas, beans, corn and cashew sauce. Repeat layers until all the ingredients are used.
3. Bake for 25 minutes. Serve topped with green onions.

Nutritional info (per serving): 239 calories; 20.6 g fat; 9.7 g carbohydrate; 8.3 g protein

Tomato Basil Soup

Cooking time: 5 minutes   **Servings:** 3

Ingredients:

- 7 cups canned tomatoes
- 3 cloves of garlic, minced
- 1 onion, chopped
- 1 cup basil
- ½ cup cashews
- 3 tablespoons nutritional yeast
- 1 tablespoon olive oil
- A pinch red pepper flakes
- Vegan cashew cream, for serving
- Salt, pepper, to taste

Instructions:

1. Preheat oil in a pan and add onion and garlic. Cook for 2-3 minutes.
2. Add tomatoes and basil, cook for 1 minute. Let cool a bit and transfer to a blender, process until smooth. Return to the pan.
3. Season with salt, pepper and red pepper flakes, cook for 3 minutes. Serve topped with cream.

Nutritional info (per serving): 198 calories; 9 g fat; 26 g carbohydrate; 5 g protein

Vegan Club Sandwich

Cooking time: 55 minutes   **Servings:** 2

Ingredients:

Sweet Potato Chips:
- 1 small sweet potato, thickly sliced
- 1 tablespoon mustard
- 1 tablespoon maple syrup
- Salt, black pepper, to taste

Miso Tahini Tofu:
- 4 oz. extra firm tofu
- ½ teaspoon miso paste
- 3 tablespoons tahini
- 1 teaspoon maple syrup
- 1 tablespoon water

For serving:
- 3 slices of bread, toasted
- ½ ripe avocado, sliced
- 1 kale leaf, washed, de-stemmed, and ripped into smaller pieces
- 1 roma tomato, thinly sliced

Instructions:

1. Preheat the oven to 375F. Arrange potato slices on the bottom of a baking dish in one layer.
2. Mix mustard, maple syrup, salt, and pepper in a bowl, and spread on top of potato chips. Bake for 20-30 minutes.
3. Pat dry tofu with paper towel. Mix miso paste, tahini, maply syrup and water in a bowl. Add tofu, toss well to coat and marinate for at least 10 minutes.
4. Place tofu on a baking tray in one layer and cook for 20-25 minutes.
5. Place avocado slices on top of each bread slice, top with kale and tomato, baked tofu and potato chips. Top with final piece of toast. Serve.

Nutritional info (per serving): 423 calories; 26.7 g fat; 38.9 g carbohydrate; 13.6 g protein

Creamy Red Pepper Alfredo Pasta

Cooking time: 10 minutes   **Servings:** 5

Ingredients:

- 1 red bell pepper, chopped
- ½ cup water
- ½ cup raw cashews
- ¼ cup nutritional yeast
- ¼ teaspoon onion powder
- ¼ teaspoon ground turmeric
- 1/8 teaspoon ground nutmeg
- 10 oz pasta of choice, cooked

Instructions:

1. Soak nuts in water for at least 6-8 hours. Drain and pat dry.
2. Add nuts, bell pepper, water, yeast, onion powder, ground turmeric and ground nutmeg to a blender and process until smooth.
3. Add sauce to a pan and preheat over medium heat. Cook for 1-2 minutes until hot.
4. Pour the sauce over pasta, toss well to coat and serve.

Nutritional info (per serving): 279 calories; 8.2 g fat; 41.2 g carbohydrate; 12.5 g protein

Sesame Noodles

Cooking time: 15 minutes **Servings:** 4

Ingredients:

- 8 oz noodles of choice, uncooked
- 3 tablespoons rice vinegar
- 3 tablespoons coconut aminos
- 1 ½ tablespoons toasted sesame oil
- 2 tablespoons honey
- 1 tablespoon garlic, minced
- ¼ teaspoon ground ginger
- Sliced scallions, for serving
- Sesame seeds, for serving

Instructions:

1. Fill a medium sauce pan with water, add salt and bring to a boil. Add noodles and cook for 6-8 minutes. Drain the noodles.
2. Mix vinegar, sesame oil, coconut aminos, honey, garlic and ginger in a bowl.
3. Pour the sauce over pasta and toss well to coat. Serve topped with scallions and sesame seeds.

Nutritional info (per serving): 531 calories; 11.8 g fat; 60.2 g carbohydrate; 14.8 g protein

Vegan Pot Pie

Cooking time: 50 minutes   **Servings:** 4-6

Ingredients:

For the Dough:
- 2 cup flour
- ½ teaspoon baking powder
- ½ teaspoon salt
- ¼ cup canola oil
- ½ cup cold water

For the Filling:
- 1 lb meatless chicken breast, chopped
- 1 onion, diced
- 2 Yukon Gold potatoes, peeled and diced
- 2 carrots, diced
- 1 cup frozen peas
- 2 garlic cloves, minced
- 3 tablespoons canola oil
- 2 tablespoons fresh sage, chopped
- 2 teaspoons fresh thyme, chopped
- 3 tablespoons all-purpose flour
- 2 cups soy milk
- Salt, pepper, to taste

Instructions:

1. Cook the dough first: mix flour, baking powder and salt in a food processor.
2. Add oil and pulse until combined. Slowly add cold water through feed tube, pulsing constantly, until soft dough forms.
3. Form the dough into a ball, then flatten into disc. Wrap in a plastic wrap and chill for at least 30 minutes.

4. Preheat the oven to 375F. Heat oil in a sauce pan over medium heat.
5. Add onion and cook until softened for about 5 minutes. Add potatoes, carrots, garlic, sage, thyme, salt and pepper; cook for 2 minutes.
6. Add flour and cook for 1 minute more. Slowly stir in soy milk and ½ cup water, stirring constantly.
7. Add meatless chicken breasts and peas and bring everything to a boil. Reduce the heat to a simmer and cook for 2 minutes. Transfer the mixture to a glass baking dish. Cool slightly.
8. Roll out pie dough to rectangle, on lightly floured surface. Place over filling and pinching to form decorative border around edge. Cut 1 inch circular vent in centre.
9. Bake in centre of oven until golden brown on top, for about 40 minutes. Cool for 10 minutes before serving.

Nutritional info (per serving): 655 calories; 27.4 g fat; 88.1 g carbohydrate; 15.7 g protein

Vegan Spaghetti alla Puttanesca

Cooking time: 20 minutes			**Servings:** 4

Ingredients:

- 8 oz whole grain spaghetti
- 1 can (28 oz) chunky tomato sauce
- ⅓ cup Kalamata olives, chopped
- ⅓ cup capers
- 1 tablespoon Kalamata olive brine
- 1 tablespoon caper brine
- 3 garlic cloves, pressed or minced
- ¼ teaspoon red pepper flakes
- 1 tablespoon olive oil
- ½ cup fresh parsley leaves, chopped
- Salt, pepper, to taste

Instructions:

1. Mix tomato sauce, olives, capers, olive bring, caper brine, garlic and red pepper flakes in a bowl.
2. Add the mixture to a sauce pan and bring to a boil over medium heat. Reduce the heat to low and simmer for 20 minutes, stirring often.

3. Remove the sauce from heat, add olive oil and chopped parsley. Season with salt and pepper.
4. Bring a large pot of salted water to a boil and cook spaghetti according to package instructions. Drain.
5. Pour the sauce over pasta and stir to combine. Serve topped with more chopped parsley.

Nutritional info (per serving): 449 calories; 8.9 g fat; 84 g carbohydrate; 16.6 g protein

Grits with Tempeh Sausage and Brussels Sprouts

Cooking time: 25 minutes   **Servings:** 4

Ingredients:

- 8 oz tempeh, crumbled
- 1 onion, thinly sliced
- 8 oz Brussels sprouts, shredded
- 4 teaspoons vegetable oil
- 1 garlic clove, minced
- 1 teaspoon chili powder
- 1 teaspoon fennel seeds
- ¾ teaspoon smoked paprika
- ¾ cup low sodium vegetable broth
- 1 tablespoon tamari
- 2 teaspoons apple cider vinegar
- 1-2 teaspoons maple syrup (to taste)
  For the Grits:
- 3 cups water
- 1 cup white corn grits
- 1 tablespoon olive oil
- 2 tablespoons nutritional yeast
- Salt, black pepper, to taste

Instructions:

1. Preheat 2 teaspoons of oil in a skillet over medium high heat. Add the tempeh and cook for 3-4 minutes, stirring frequently.
2. Add garlic and cook for 1 more minute, stirring constantly. Add chili, fennel, paprika, broth, tamari, vinegar, and maple syrup to the skillet. Bring everything to a boil and reduce the heat to low.
3. Cook until the broth has been absorbed. Transfer the crumbles to a plate and set aside.

4. Add 2 teaspoons oil to the same skillet. Add onion and Brussels sprouts, season with salt and pepper.
5. Cook for about 6-8 minutes, stirring occasionally. Add the sausage crumbles to onions and sprouts, mix well and adjust salt and pepper to taste. Remove from heat.
6. Bring water and salt to boil. Whisk in the grits and reduce the heat to medium low. Cook for 5-10 minutes, stirring constantly. Add vegan butter and nutritional yeast.
7. Serve grits with tempeh and sausage mixture on the side.

Nutritional info (per serving): 249 calories; 14.9 g fat; 18.6 g carbohydrate; 15.8 g protein

Minestrone Soup

Cooking time: 20 minutes   **Servings:** 6

Ingredients:

- 1 white onion, diced
- 3 garlic cloves, minced
- 3 carrots, chopped
- 2 celery ribs, chopped
- 1 can (28 oz) diced tomatoes with juices
- 4 cups vegetable broth
- 1 teaspoon dried basil
- 1 teaspoon dried oregano
- 1 ¼ cup pasta of choice, uncooked
- 1 can (19 oz) kidney beans, drained and rinsed
- Salt, pepper, to taste

Instructions:

1. Add 2-3 tablespoons of water or broth to a large sauce pan and add onions, garlic, carrots and celery. Cook over medium heat for 2-3 minutes, stirring frequently.
2. Add diced tomatoes, basil, oregano, broth, beans and pasta, simmer for about 10-15 minutes.
3. Season with salt and pepper and serve hot.

Nutritional info (per serving): 315 calories; 4.1 g fat; 53.8 g carbohydrate; 12.8 g protein

Mushrooms and Peas Vegan Risotto

Cooking time: 25 minutes **Servings:** 4

Ingredients:

- 1 tablespoon olive oil
- 1 small onion, diced
- 2 garlic cloves, minced
- 1 ½ cup Arborio rice
- 4 cups vegetable broth
- ½ cup dry white wine
- ¾ cup frozen peas
- 2 tablespoons vegan butter
- Juice of one lemon
- 1 teaspoon lemon zest
- ½ teaspoon ground coriander
- 1 cup button mushrooms, sliced
- 1/3 cup vegan parmesan cheese, grated
- Salt, pepper, to taste

Instructions:

1. Add broth to a medium pan and heat it up over low heat for up to 10 minutes.
2. Heat oil in a large pan over medium heat. Add onion and garlic, cook for 4-5 minutes until onions are translucent. Add mushrooms, cook for 5 more minutes.
3. Add rice and cook for 1 more minute. Reduce heat to low.
4. Add white wine and lemon juice, Cook until almost all wine has dissolved, stir constantly.
5. Add 1 cup of vegetable broth to rice and cook until almost all broth evaporates. Add one more cup and repeat the process, until rice is soft and cooked. Add hot water to rice if you need more liquid.
6. Add peas, vegan butter, lemon zest, coriander, salt and pepper. Cook for 3-5 minutes.

7. Serve with vegan cheese on top.

Nutritional info (per serving): 386 calories; 5.4 g fat; 65.5 g carbohydrate; 12 g protein

Stewed Chickpeas and Chard Toast

Cooking time: 20 minutes **Servings:** 4

Ingredients:

- 4 slices whole-wheat bread
- 1 can (14.5-oz.) diced tomatoes, unsalted
- 8 oz rainbow chard, chopped
- 6 garlic cloves, minced
- 3 tablespoons extra-virgin olive oil
- 1 cup yellow onion, chopped
- 1 teaspoon ground cumin
- ¾ teaspoon smoked paprika
- ¼ teaspoon crushed red pepper
- 1 can (15 oz) chickpeas, drained
- Salt, to taste

Instructions:

1. Preheat the broiler. Add tomatoes to a food processor and pulse until pureed.
2. Preheat 2 tablespoons oil in a skillet over medium heat. Add onion and garlic, cook for about 3 minutes.
3. Add chard and cook for 3 minutes, stirring occasionally. Add cumin, paprika, red pepper and salt, cook for about 30 seconds.
4. Add chickpeas and tomatoes and bring to a simmer. Reduce the heat to low and cover the skillet. Cook for about 5 minutes.
5. Place bread slices on a baking tray in one layer.
6. Cut remaining garlic clove in half. Place bread in a single layer on a baking sheet. Broil for about 1 minute. Turn bread over; brush with 1 tablespoon oil.
7. Top each slice with about 1 cup of chickpea mixture.

Nutritional info (per serving): 352 calories; 13 g fat; 48 g carbohydrate; 13 g protein

Broccoli Quinoa Gratin

Cooking time: 20 minutes   **Servings:** 4

Ingredients:

- 1 cup quinoa, rinsed
- 2 cups vegetable broth
- 1 cup soy or almond milk
- 1 can (15 oz) chickpeas
- 1 broccoli head, broken into florets
- 1 teaspoon onion powder
- 1 teaspoon ground oregano
- ¾ teaspoon paprika
- 1 tablespoon oil
- 3 tablespoons oats
- 1 tablespoon nutritional yeast flakes
- A pinch of turmeric
- 1 teaspoon soy sauce
- ½ teaspoon smoked paprika
- 7 oz vegan cheese sauce
- Salt, pepper, to taste

Instructions:

1. Preheat the oven to 400F.
2. Add vegetable broth to a sauce pan and bring to a boil. Add quinoa and simmer for 15-20 minutes.
3. Spread broccoli florets on a baking sheet in one layer, drizzle with little oil and season with salt. Bake for about 15 minutes.
4. Add oats, nutritional yeast, onion powder, 1 tablespoon oil, paprika, turmeric, soy sauce, salt and pepper to a bowl and mix well to combine.
5. Preheat oil in a sauce pan over medium heat, add breadcrumbs mixture, cook for about 30 seconds-1 minute.
6. Add 1 cup milk, remaining spices, chickpeas and half of the cheese sauce to quinoa and stir well.
7. Transfer the mixture into a lightly greased casserole dish, add broccoli florets and spread the rest of the cheese on top. Sprinkle with the "breadcrumbs".

8. Bake the casserole for about 10-15 minutes.

Nutritional info (per serving): 443 calories; 15.6 g fat; 47 g carbohydrate; 19 g protein

Vegan Spinach Artichoke Quesadillas

Cooking time: 8 minutes   **Servings:** 2-4

Ingredients:

- 2-4 flour tortillas
- 3 cups baby spinach
- 1 garlic clove, diced
- ½ teaspoon olive oil
- 6 oz marinated artichoke hearts, diced
- 4 oz vegan cream cheese
- 2 tablespoons vegan mayo
- Salt and pepper, to taste

Instructions:

1. Preheat olive oil in a pan over medium heat. Add garlic and cook for 1 minute, stirring frequently.
2. Add artichoke hearts and 2 cups of spinach. Stir well to combine and cook until spinach begins to wilt.
3. Add cream cheese, mayo, salt and pepper and stir to combine. Cook for 1 minute and set aside.
4. Preheat a big non stick pan over medium heat. Place 1 tortilla into the pan and fill with part of the spinach mixture. Add additional spinach on top. Fold tortilla in half and cook until bottom begins to brown, for about 2 minutes.
5. Flip and cook for 1 minute more. Repeat with the rest of tortillas.

Nutritional info (per serving): 128 calories; 9 g fat; 9.7 g carbohydrate; 2.6 g protein

Quinoa and Roasted Pepper Chili

Cooking time: 25 minutes   **Servings:** 4

Ingredients:

- 1/3 cup quinoa, uncooked, rinsed
- 1 can (14.5 oz) fire-roasted diced tomatoes with chipotles, undrained
- 1 can (15 oz) pinto beans, rinsed and drained
- 1 cup low-sodium vegetable broth
- 2 bell peppers, halved lengthwise, deseeded
- 2 poblano chiles, halved lengthwise, deseeded
- 4 teaspoons olive oil
- 3 cups zucchini, chopped
- 1 ½ cups onion, chopped
- 4 garlic cloves, minced
- 1 tablespoon chili powder
- 1 teaspoon ground cumin
- ½ teaspoon smoked paprika
- ½ cup water
- Salt, pepper, to taste

Instructions:

1. Preheat broiler.
2. Place bell pepper and chiles halves on a baking sheet lined with foil, skin sides up. Broil for 10 minutes. Place roasted peppers to a paper bag; close tightly. Let stand for 10 minutes. Peel and chop.
3. Preheat a large skillet over medium heat. Add oil, zucchini, onion and garlic, cook for 4 minutes.
4. Add chili powder, cumin and paprika, sauté for 30 seconds. Add peppers and chiles, water and remaining ingredients; bring to a boil.
5. Reduce heat to low, cover the pan and cook for 20 minutes.

Nutritional info (per serving): 258 calories; 6.3 g fat; 42.1 g carbohydrate; 9.7 g protein

Ratatouille

Cooking time: 20 minutes   **Servings:** 4

Ingredients:

- 1 onion, diced
- 2 bell peppers, better of different color, chopped
- 1 eggplant, cut into cubes
- 2 tomatoes, cut into large cubes
- 1 zucchini, sliced
- 4 garlic cloves, minced
- 1 tablespoon olive oil
- 1 bay leaf
- ½ cup tomato juice
- 5 tablespoons tomato paste
- 4 tablespoons dry red wine
- 1 teaspoon dried basil
- ½ teaspoon dried oregano
- ½ teaspoon dried rosemary
- ½ teaspoon dried marjoram
- Salt, pepper, to taste

Instructions:

1. Heat oil in a pan over medium heat. Add onion and sauté for 4-5 minutes until translucent.
2. Add red wine, bay leaf and tomato juice, mix well until combined.
3. Add basil, oregano, rosemary, marjoram, garlic, salt and pepper, stir well. Cover the pan and cook over low heat for 10 minutes.
4. Add zucchini and bell peppers, cook for 5 more minutes. Then add tomatoes, tomato paste and eggplant. Cover the pan and cook for 8-10 minutes.
5. Turn off the heat, stir the veggies and allow to cool a little before serving.

Nutritional info (per serving): 170 calories; 4 g fat; 31 g carbohydrate; 6 g protein

Vegan Meatballs

Cooking time: 45 minutes   **Servings:** 12

Ingredients:

- 1 cup quinoa, cooked and cooled
- 1 can (15 oz) black beans, rinsed, drained and dried
- 2 tablespoons avocado oil
- 3 garlic cloves, minced
- ½ cup shallot, diced
- 2 ½ teaspoons fresh oregano
- ½ teaspoon red pepper flakes
- ½ cup vegan parmesan cheese
- 2 tablespoons tomato paste
- 3 tablespoons fresh basil, chopped
- 2 tablespoons vegan Worcestershire sauce
- Salt, to taste

Instructions:

1. Preheat the oven to 350F.
2. Spread beans on a baking tray lined with parchment paper. Bake for 15 minutes. Remove from the oven and increase the temperature to 375F.
3. Preheat oil in a large skillet over medium heat. Add garlic and shallot, sauté for 2-3 minutes.
4. Add black beans, cooked garlic and shallots, oregano, red pepper flakes and salt to a food processor. Blend until loose. Add quinoa, vegan parmesan cheese, tomato paste, fresh basil and Worcestershire sauce. Pulse until combined.
5. Form the mixture into balls. Add to a plate and refrigerate for 15 minutes.
6. Preheat non stick skillet and add balls, sauté for couple of minutes until lightly brown on all sides. Transfer to a baking dish and bake for 20-30 minutes.

Nutritional info (per serving): 67.4 calories; 1.9 g fat; 10 g carbohydrate; 3.3 g protein

Creamed Spinach

Cooking time: 10 minutes   **Servings:** 2

Ingredients:

- 3 lbs fresh spinach, chopped
- ½ cup soy milk
- 1 ¼ cups water
- 1 package onion soup mix
- 1 teaspoon nutritional yeast

Instructions:

1. Add water to a medium sauce pan and bring to a boil. Add onion soup mix and stir well to combine, until dissolved.
2. Add spinach and reduce the heat to low. Cook for about 5 minutes, stirring occasionally.
3. Add soy milk and stir for a few minutes.
4. In a medium-sized saucepan, bring the water to a simmer and add the entire packet of onion soup or dip mix, stirring well to combine. Add nutritional yeast and stir well.
5. Remove from heat and serve.

Nutritional info (per serving): 83 calories; 6 g fat; 5 g carbohydrate; 3 g protein

Vegan Burrito

Cooking time: 10 minutes

Servings: 4-6

Ingredients:

- 4-5 large flour tortillas
- 1 can (15 oz) black beans, drained and rinsed
- 1 ½ cups white rice, cooked
- ½ cup corn kernels, canned
- ½ cup romaine lettuce, chopped
- 1 medium tomato, chopped
- 1 tablespoon extra virgin olive oil
- 1 teaspoon ground cumin
- 1 teaspoon dried oregano
- ¼ teaspoon garlic powder
- A pinch red pepper flakes
- 2 tablespoons fresh cilantro, chopped
- 1 avocado, mashed with a fork
- Salt, pepper, to taste

Instructions:

1. Preheat oil in a skillet, add beans, cumin, oregano, garlic powder, red pepper flakes, salt and pepper. Stir well and cook for 3-5 minutes.
2. Place tortilla on a work surface, stuff each tortilla with rice, beans, corn, lettuce, tomato, cilantro and avocado. Fold in the sides and roll up, then wrap in foil.
3. Cook the burritos in a skillet over medium heat for about 2-3 minutes on each side. Serve hot.

Nutritional info (per serving): 534 calories; 21.6 g fat; 75.1 g carbohydrate; 15.7 g protein

Tacos

Cooking time: 15 minutes   **Servings:** 12-16

Ingredients:

- 12-16 corn tortillas
- ½ onion, chopped
- 1 can (15 oz) black beans, drained
- 1 tablespoon olive oil
- 1 teaspoon crushed garlic
- ½ teaspoon ground cumin
- 2-3 cups salsa
- 1 cup tahini
- ¼ teaspoon cayenne pepper
- ¼ teaspoon chili flakes
- ½ teaspoon ground cumin
- 2–3 cups lettuce, shredded
- 2 avocados, peeled and chopped
- Salt, pepper, to taste

Instructions:

1. Preheat oil in a pan over medium heat, add onion, garlic, cayenne pepper, chili flakes and ground cumin, cook for 3-4 minutes.
2. Add black beans and cook for 1-2 minutes. Season with salt and pepper.
3. Stack the tortillas and cover with foil. Preheat in the oven at 350F for about 15 minutes.
4. Spread lettuce on each tortilla, top with beans, salsa, avocado and tahini sauce. Serve.

Nutritional info (per serving): 325 calories; 14.9 g fat; 42.2 g carbohydrate; 10.1 g protein

Pepperoni Pizza

Cooking time: 15 minutes   **Servings:** 2

Ingredients:

- 8 oz flour
- ½ cup water
- 1 tablespoon olive oil
- 2 teaspoons baking powder
- 2 tablespoons tomato paste
- 2 zucchini, thinly sliced
- ½ tomato, sliced
- ½ red onion, sliced
- ½ teaspoon hot sauce
- 2 tablespoons tamari
- 2 tablespoons balsamic vinegar
- Vegan cheese
- Salt, to taste

Instructions:

1. Mix hot sauce, tamari and vinegar in a bowl. Add zucchini and mix well to coat. Cover the bowl and marinate overnight in the fridge.
2. Mix flour, water, oil, baking powder and salt in a bowl, knead well. Let rest for 2-3 minutes.
3. Form the pizza crust, spread the dough on the working surface.
4. Preheat the oven to 390F.
5. Spread the tomato paste on top of the crust. Add marinated zucchini slices, tomato and onion. Top with vegan cheese.
6. Bake for 12-15 minutes.

Nutritional info (per serving): 536 calories; 8.69 g fat; 99.7 g carbohydrate; 16.7 g protein

Spinach Artichoke Pizza

Cooking time: 5 minutes   **Servings:** 12

Ingredients:

- 2 pre-made pizza dough
- 1 can artichoke hearts, drained, quartered
- 1 onion, chopped
- 5 cups fresh spinach
- 2 garlic cloves, minced
- 1 can white beans, rinsed and drained
- ¼ cup water
- 2 tablespoons nutritional yeast
- ½ cup cashews
- 1 tablespoon fresh lemon juice
- ½ cup vegan mozzarella cheese
- Salt, pepper, to taste

Instructions:

1. Preheat the oven to 350 F. Add beans, cashews, lemon juice, water and the yeast to a blender. Process until smooth.
2. Preheat oil in a pan and cook for about 3 minutes. Add garlic, 2 cups of spinach and cook for 3 minutes. Add processed white beans mixture, season with salt and pepper.
3. Spread the mixture on pizza dough, top with artichoke hearts and the remaining spinach. Sprinkle with cheese.
4. Bake for 8 minutes and serve.

Nutritional info (per serving): 177 calories; 6 g fat; 26 g carbohydrate; 7 g protein

Mushroom Bean Burger

Cooking time: 10 minutes   **Servings:** 5-6

Ingredients:

- ¾ cup mushrooms, diced
- 1 can (15 oz) pinto beans
- 3 tablespoons oil
- 1 onion, diced
- 1 garlic clove, minced
- 3 green onions, diced
- ½ teaspoon cumin
- 1 teaspoon parsley
- Salt, pepper, to taste

For Serving:
- Burger buns
- Sliced cucumber
- Tomato, sliced

Instructions:

1. Preheat 1 tablespoon oil in a skillet, add onion and garlic, cook for 3-5 minutes.
2. Add green onions, cumin and mushrooms and cook for 5 minutes.
3. Mash the beans with a fork, add onion mushroom mixture, parsley, salt and pepper. Mix well to combine.
4. Shape the mixture into patties. Heat 2 tablespoons oil in a skillet and cook patties for about 3 minutes on each side.
5. Serve patties on buns with cucumber and tomato.

Nutritional info (per serving): 313 calories; 4 g fat; 55 g carbohydrate; 18 g protein

Vegan Jambalaya

Cooking time: 30 minutes   **Servings:** 6-8

Ingredients:

- 1 cup rice, uncooked
- 3 cups water
- 1 cup canned chickpeas
- 1 cup canned kidney beans
- ½ onion, chopped
- 2 garlic cloves, chopped
- 1 bell pepper, chopped
- 1 carrot, chopped
- 1 can (14 oz) chopped tomatoes
- 2 tablespoons tamari sauce
- 2 teaspoons dried oregano
- 1 teaspoon dried thyme
- 1 teaspoon garlic powder
- 1 teaspoon onion powder
- 1 teaspoon cumin powder
- 1 teaspoon paprika
- 1/8 teaspoon cayenne powder
- Chopped fresh parsley, for serving
- Salt, pepper, to taste

Instructions:

1. Add all the vegetables to the sauce pan along with 3 tablespoons water. Cook for about 5 minutes.
2. Add tomatoes and cook for another 5 minutes. Add tamari and all the spices to the pan, stir well to combine.
3. Add rice and 3 cups water and bring to a boil. Cover and cook on medium high for 15 minutes.
4. Add tahini, chickpeas and beans, cook for 1-2 minutes. Serve with parsley on top.

Nutritional info (per serving): 305 calories; 4.1 g fat; 53.9 g carbohydrate; 13.8 g protein

Creamy Lemon Pepper Chickpeas

Cooking time: 15 minutes   **Servings:** 4

Ingredients:

- 1 can (19 oz) chickpeas, drained and rinsed
- ¼ cup full fat coconut milk
- 1 tablespoon olive oil
- ½ onion, chopped
- 3 garlic cloves, minced
- 1 tablespoon flour
- 1 cup vegetable broth
- 1 lemon, zested
- 2 tablespoons lemon juice
- A handful cilantro, chopped
- Salt, pepper, to taste

Instructions:

1. Preheat oil in a skillet over medium heat. Add onions and garlic, cook for about 5 minutes.
2. Add flour and cook for 30 seconds more. Add broth, lemon juice, lemon zest, salt, and pepper. Deglaze the pan.
3. Add chickpeas and bring to a boil. Cook for 5-10 minutes.
4. Add coconut milk and stir well to combine. Serve topped with cilantro.

Nutritional info (per serving): 229 calories; 9.5 g fat; 30.1 g carbohydrate; 8.5 g protein

Potato Pancakes

Cooking time: 10 minutes   **Servings:** 10-12

Ingredients:

- 3 yukon gold potatoes, grated
- ½ yellow onion, grated
- ½ cup flour
- 2 green onions, chopped
- 2 garlic cloves, minced
- 1 Jalapeno, minced
- ¼ teaspoon baking powder
- 2-3 tablespoons oil
- Salt, pepper, to taste

Instructions:

1. Mix potatoes, onion, flour, green onions, garlic, Jalapeno, baking powder, salt and pepper in a bowl.
2. Add oil to a skillet and preheat over medium heat. Add about 1-2 tablespoons of potato mixture to the pan and form into patty. Cook for about 2 minutes per side. Repeat until all the mixture is used. Serve.

Nutritional info (per serving): 69 calories; 1 g fat; 12 g carbohydrate; 2 g protein

Tofu and Cauliflower Balti

Cooking time: 35 minutes   **Servings:** 4

Ingredients:

- 1 pack tofu, drained and pressed, cut into cubes
- 2 tablespoons oil
- 3 tablespoons flour
- ½ cauliflower head, cut into florets
- 1 cup vegetable stock
- ½ tablespoon garam masala
- 1 teaspoon coriander seeds
- 1 teaspoon cumin seeds
- 1 teaspoon mustard seeds
- 1 teaspoon fennel seeds
- 6 cardamon pods
- ¼ teaspoon cloves
- 2 bay leaves
- 1 teaspoon turmeric
- 2 tablespoons tomato puree
- 1 teaspoon ground ginger
- 2 garlic cloves
- 2 tablespoons coconut oil
- 1 – inch piece ginger, grated
- Salt, pepper, to taste

Instructions:

1. Dust tofu cubes in flour. Preheat 1 tablespoon oil in a skillet and cook tofu for 5 minutes.
2. Add coriander seeds, cumin seeds, mustard seeds, fennel seeds, cardamom pods and bay leaves to a non stick frying pan. Dry fry for 1-2 minutes. Transfer to a blender and process until smooth.
3. Mix the processed spices, turmeric, curry powder, ground ginger, puree, vinegar, coconut oil, garlic and ginger in a bowl. Stir into a paste.
4. Add about 1 tablespoon oil to a pan, heat over medium heat. Add tofu and cauliflower, cook for 3 minutes. Add stock, salt and pepper and cook for 10 minutes.

5. Add garam masala and fresh coriander, stir, cooking for 3 minutes. Serve over rice.

Nutritional info (per serving): 183 calories; 15.2 g fat; 9.6 g carbohydrate; 4 g protein

Coconut Apple Ginger Dal

Cooking time: 20 minutes　　**Servings:** 4

Ingredients:

- 1 piece (3-inch) ginger, peeled, chopped
- 1 apple, grated
- 1 ½ cups lentils
- 1 can (13.5 oz) coconut milk
- ½ onion, chopped
- 2 garlic cloves, chopped
- 2 tablespoons virgin coconut oil
- ¼ teaspoon cayenne pepper
- ¼ teaspoon ground cumin
- ¼ teaspoon ground turmeric
- 2 tablespoons fresh lime juice
- 2 ½ cups water
- Salt, pepper, to taste

Instructions:

1. Preheat oil in a pot over medium heat. Add cayenne, cumin and turmeric, cook for about 1 minute, stirring.
2. Add onion, garlic and ginger, cook for 3 minutes. Add apple and lentils and stir to combine everything.
3. Add coconut milk and water, bring everything to a boil. Reduce the heat to low and cook for 20-25 minutes, stirring occasionally.
4. Season with salt and pepper and add lime juice. Serve.

Nutritional info (per serving): 430 calories; 15.2 g fat; 56.3 g carbohydrate; 20.4 g protein

Vegetable Risotto

Cooking time: 25 minutes   **Servings:** 4

Ingredients:

- 3.5-4 cups vegetable broth
- 2 tablespoons water (or oil), divided
- 1 small bundle asparagus, ends trimmed (or 1 small bundle broccolini, stalks trimmed (or use both)
- 1 medium red bell pepper, seeds and stems removed, thinly sliced
- 1/4 teaspoon sea salt
- 1/4 teaspoon black pepper
- 3/4 cup thinly sliced shallot
- 1 cup arborio rice
- 1/4 cup dry white wine (or sub more vegetable broth)
- 1/4 cup vegan parmesan cheese (plus more for serving)
- fresh chopped parsley, for serving (optional)

Instructions:

1. Put vegetable broth into a medium saucepan and heat it on a medium heat. Then once simmering, reduce the heat to low to keep warm.
2. Preheat a large pan on a medium heat, and once hot, add half of water (or oil), asparagus (and/or broccolini) and red bell pepper. Then season with a pinch of salt and pepper.
3. Sauté for 3-4 minutes stirring frequently until just tender and slightly browned. Then cover to steam and speed the cooking time, and remove from the pan, uncover, and set aside.

4. Preheat another large rimmed pan on a medium heat, and once hot, add the remaining water (or oil), shallot and sauté for 1-2 minutes or until softened and very slightly browned.
5. Add arborio rice and cook for 1 minute, stirring occasionally. Then add dry white wine (or more vegetable broth) and stir gently, cook for 1-2 minutes or until the liquid is absorbed.
6. By using a ladle, add warmed vegetable broth 1/2 cup at a time, stirring almost constantly, giving the risotto little breaks to come back to a simmer (the heat should be medium, and there should always be a slight simmer, and you want the mixture to be cooking but not boiling or it will get gummy and cook too fast).
7. Continue to add vegetable broth 1 ladle at a time, stirring to incorporate, until the rice is cooked through, but not mushy (the whole process should only take 15-20 minutes and may take longer if making a larger batch).
8. Once the rice is cooked through, remove it from heat and season with salt and pepper to taste. Also add vegan parmesan cheese and most of the cooked vegetables, reserving a few for serving. Stir to coat.
9. Taste and adjust flavor as needed, adding a pinch of salt and pepper to taste or more vegan parmesan to enhance the cheesiness.

Nutritional info (per serving): 257 calories; 2.2 g fat; 50 g carbohydrate; 5.7 g protein

Coconut Curry Ramen

Cooking time: 1 hour 15 minutes   **Servings:** 4

Ingredients:

- 2 tablespoons toasted or untoasted sesame oil
- 2 small knobs ginger, sliced lengthwise into long strips
- 10 cloves garlic, chopped
- 2 large onions, chopped lengthwise
- 5 tablespoons yellow or green curry paste
- 8 cups vegetable broth
- 4 cups light coconut milk
- 2-4 tablespoons coconut sugar (optional)
- 1 teaspoon ground turmeric (optional)
- 2 tablespoons white or yellow miso paste
- 4-6 cups noodles of choice
- fresh green onion, chopped (optional)
- sriracha or chili garlic sauce (optional)

Instructions:

1. Preheat a large pot on a medium-high heat, and once hot, add oil, garlic, ginger, onion.
2. Sauté stirring occasionally for 5-8 minutes or until the onion has browned edges.
3. Then add curry paste and sauté for 1-2 minutes more, stirring frequently.
4. Add vegetable broth and coconut milk and stir to deglaze the bottom of the pan.
5. Bring to a simmer on a medium heat, reduce the heat to low and cover. Simmer on low for at least 1 hour, stirring occasionally (the longer it cooks, the more the flavor will deepen and develop).

6. Taste broth and adjust the seasonings as needed, adding coconut sugar for a little sweetness, turmeric for more intense curry flavor, or more sesame oil for nuttiness.
7. About 10 minutes before serving, prepare any desired toppings/sides, such as noodles, or green onion (optional).
8. Just before serving, scoop out 1/2 cup of the broth and whisk in the miso paste. Once fully dissolved, add back to the pot and turn off the heat and stir to combine.
9. Either strain broth through a fine mesh strainer (discard onions and ginger or add back to the soup) or ladle out the broth and leave the onions and mushrooms behind.
10. To serve, divide noodles of choice between the serving bowls. Top with broth and desired toppings. Serve with chili garlic sauce or sriracha sauce.

Nutritional info (per serving): 417 calories; 19.4 g fat; 56 g carbohydrate; 8.9 g protein

Sweet Potato Noodle Pasta

Cooking time: 10 minutes   **Servings:** 4

Ingredients:

For the sauce:

- 1 cup raw cashews
- 3 cloves garlic (add more or less to taste for preferred garlicky flavor)
- 4-5 tablespoons nutritional yeast
- 1/2 teaspoon sea salt
- 2 teaspoon arrowroot starch (or cornstarch; for thickening)
- 1.5-2 cups unsweetened plain almond or rice milk (more as needed)
- 1 pinch red pepper flake (optional)

For noodles:

- 3 medium sweet potatoes, peeled and spiralized
- fresh parsley, chopped (for serving, optional)
- sautéed kale or kale chips (for serving, optional)
- crispy chickpeas (for serving, optional)
- vegan parmesan cheese (for serving, optional)
- red pepper flakes (for serving, optional)

Instructions:

1. Put cashews into a small mixing bowl and soak for 30 minutes in a very hot water. Then drain thoroughly and set aside. (Or soak cashews overnight or 6-8 hours in cool water).
2. If serving with kale chips or sautéed kale (or crispy chickpeas), prepare now and set aside until serving.
3. Once cashews are ready, peel and spiralize potatoes. Set aside.
4. Put drained cashews, garlic, nutritional yeast, salt, arrowroot starch, and almond or rice milk into a high-speed blender.
5. Blend on high until creamy and smooth, scraping the sides as needed. Taste and adjust the flavor. If too thick, thin with a bit more almond milk.
6. Put sauce into a large, rimmed pan or pot and heat on a medium-low heat constantly whisling until it starts bubbling. Once bubbling, reduce the heat to a very low simmer to keep warm. If too thick, thin with a bit more almond milk.
7. Pour 1 inch water to a large pot, put a steamer basket on top and heat on a medium-high heat until it starts bubbling. Once bubbling, add potato noodles, cover to steam for 3-5 minutes or until cooked or soften a bit (depending on taste).
8. Add sweet potatoes to the sauce and gently toss to combine. If using kale or other add-ins, this the time to add.
9. Serve as is or garnish with fresh parsley, crispy chickpeas, kale, vegan parmesan, or red pepper flake (optional).

Nutritional info (per serving): 417 calories; 19.4 g fat; 56 g carbohydrate; 8.9 g protein

Vegan Poutine

Cooking time: 45 minutes **Servings:** 6

Ingredients:

For the fries:

- 4 medium russet potatoes, unpeeled (or sub sweet potatoes for a savory-sweet poutine)
- 3-4 tablespoons avocado or melted coconut oil
- 1/2 teaspoon sea salt

For the gravy:

- 3 tablespoons avocado or melted coconut oil
- 2 medium shallots (minced)
- 1 1/2 cups diced button or cremini mushrooms
- 1/4 teaspoon each sea salt and black pepper (plus more to taste)
- 1 tablespoon balsamic vinegar
- 1 teaspoon coconut aminos (optional)
- 3 tablespoons cornstarch (or arrowroot)
- 1/2 cup vegetable broth
- 1 cup unsweetened plain almond milk
- 1-2 teaspoon vegan Worcestershire sauce or ketchup (optional)
- 1 batch vegan mozzarella cheese", separated into 1 teaspoon amounts

Instructions:

1. Chop potatoes into thin slices by halving lengthwise and cutting into wedges and strips. For wedges, cut into larger pieces.

2. Line two large baking sheets with parchment paper, then put fries, oil, salt and toss to coat. Arrange fries in a single layer, making sure they aren't overlapping too much.
3. Preheat the oven to 450F and bake for a total of 25-35 minutes, tossing/flipping at least once to ensure even baking. Once cooked, remove from oven and set aside.
4. Prepare the gravy by heating a rimmed skillet on a medium heat. Once hot, add oil (or water), shallots and sauté for 2-3 minutes, stirring occasionally.
5. Then add mushrooms, salt, pepper, balsamic vinegar, and coconut aminos (optional). Stir.
6. Increase the heat to a medium high to brown mushrooms, cook for 4-5 minutes or until slightly caramelized. Add cornstarch and stir to coat.
7. Lower the heat to low and slowly add broth and almond milk while whisking. Cook for 4-5 minutes, or until you've reached the desired consistency. If too thick, thin with a bit more almond milk.
8. Put into a blender and blend until smooth. Taste and adjust the flavor as needed
9. Return gravy to stovetop and heat on a lowest heat to keep warm.

Nutritional info (per serving): 432 calories; 28.4 g fat; 40.3 g carbohydrate; 7.5 g protein

Cauliflower Rice Kitchari

Cooking time: 45 minutes   **Servings**: 4

Ingredients:

- 3/4 cup moong dal or chana dal
- 1.5 tablespoons coconut or avocado oil
- 1.5 teaspoon cumin seed
- 1 teaspoon mustard seed
- 2 tablespoons grated (or finely chopped) ginger
- 1-2 small serrano peppers, seeds removed, diced
- 1/4 teaspoon asafoetida
- 1 cup diced tomatoes
- 2 cups water
- 2 whole cloves (optional)
- 2 whole cardamom pods (optional)
- 2 cups cauliflower rice
- 1/2 teaspoon garam masala
- 1 teaspoon ground cumin
- 1 teaspoon ground turmeric (plus more to taste)
- 2-3 tablespoons coconut aminos (plus more to taste)
- 1/4 teaspoon sea salt (plus more to taste)
- 1/3 cup light coconut milk (optional)

Instructions:

1. Put moong dal (or chana dal) into a large pot or a skillet, top with cold water and soak overnight (or for 6 hours). Once soaked, rinse, drain and set aside in strainer.

2. Heat the same large pot or rimmed skillet on a medium heat, and once hot, add oil (or water), cumin seed, mustard seed, ginger, serrano peppers, asafoetida, and tomatoes. Sauté for a few minutes, stirring occasionally.
3. Next, add moong dal and sauté for a few minutes, stirring occasionally. Then add water, clove (optional), and cardamom (optional). Increase the heat and bring to a low boil.
4. Then reduce the heat to a simmer, cover, and cook for about 15-20 minutes until moong dal is tender.
5. Add cauliflower rice, garam masala, cumin, turmeric, coconut aminos, sea salt and stir to combine. Cover and cook for about 10-15 minutes stirring occasionally until cauliflower rice is tender. If the mixture becomes too dry, add more water.
6. Add coconut milk at this time for creamier texture (optional). Taste and adjust the flavor as needed.
7. Serve as is or over rice, greens, or roasted vegetables.

Nutritional info (per serving): 270 calories; 5.7 g fat; 40 g carbohydrate; 15.7 g protein

Moroccan-Spiced Eggplant and Tomato Stew

Cooking time: 50 minutes

Servings: 4

Ingredients:

- 1 large eggplant (7 cups), unpeeled and cut into bite-size pieces
- 2 tablespoons olive or melted coconut oil
- 1/2 teaspoon sea salt
- 2 tablespoons olive or coconut oil
- 1 large white or yellow onion, thinly sliced
- 3 cloves garlic, minced
- 1 tablespoon ground cumin
- 1 tablespoon smoked paprika
- 1/4 teaspoon sea salt (plus more to taste)
- 2 cans (14.5-oz) diced fire-roasted tomatoes
- 1/2 cup water (or vegetable broth)
- 1 cup cooked chickpeas, well rinsed and drained (optional)
- 1 tablespoon maple syrup or coconut sugar
- 2 tablespoons harissa paste
- cilantro or parsley
- white rice, brown rice, or quinoa (or sub cauliflower rice* for grain-free)
- fresh lemon

Instructions:

1. Preheat the oven to 425F and line a large baking sheet with parchment paper.
2. Put diced eggplant, drizzle with avocado or olive oil, sprinkle with salt and toss to coat and roast for 30-35 minutes, flipping/tossing near the 20-minute mark.
3. Heat a large rimmed pan or pot on a medium heat, and once hot, add oil (or water) and onions. Sauté for 4-5 minutes, stirring frequently, or until soft and slightly caramelized.

4. Add garlic, cumin, paprika and stir to coat. Cook for 1 more minute.
5. Add tomatoes and their juices as well as water (or vegetable broth). Cover and bring to a simmer on a medium heat, and cook for 4 minutes to allow flavors to develop.
6. Remove the cover and add rinsed and drained chickpeas (optional), maple syrup, harissa paste and stir to coat. Then cover and simmer on a medium-low heat.
7. Remove the roasted eggplant from the oven, turn the oven off, and add eggplant to the tomatoes and chickpeas. Stir to combine and cover. Simmer on a medium-low/low heat for another 10 minutes to allow flavors to deepen.
8. Taste and adjust the flavors as needed.
9. Serve as is or over rice or grain of choice (or pasta or roasted vegetables) with wedges of fresh lemon and fresh chopped parsley or cilantro.

Nutritional info (per serving): 240 calories; 14.1 g fat; 25.7 g carbohydrate; 2.2 g protein

Red Curry with Roasted Vegetables

Cooking time: 25 minutes   **Servings**: 4

Ingredients:

- 1 large sweet potato, cubed, skin on
- 2 cups broccoli or cauliflower, chopped, large stems removed
- 1 1/2 cups red cabbage, sliced
- 1 tablespoon neutral oil, divided
- 1 tablespoon maple syrup
- 1 teaspoon curry powder
- 1/4 teaspoon sea salt
- 2 tablespoons coconut oil
- 2/3 cup shallot, chopped
- 6 cloves garlic, minced
- 5 tablespoons ginger, freshly minced
- 6 tablespoons red curry paste
- 2 cans (14-oz) light coconut milk
- 1 healthy pinch sea salt (plus more to taste)
- 1/2 teaspoon ground turmeric
- 2 tablespoons maple syrup
- 2 tablespoons coconut aminos (or sub tamari or soy sauce if not gluten-free)
- 2 tablespoons lime juice (plus more to taste)
- cauliflower rice, quinoa, or rice
- cilantro
- lime wedges

Instructions:

1. Preheat the oven to 375F and line a baking sheet (or more, as needed) with parchment paper.
2. Put vegetables, oil, maple syrup, curry powder, sea salt into a mixing bowl and toss.

3. Put sweet potatoes into a baking sheet (leaving broccoli and cabbage behind) and roast for 10 minutes. At the 10-minute mark, remove pan from the oven, add broccoli and cabbage and return to the oven and roast for 12-15 more minutes.
4. Prepare curry by heating a large rimmed skillet or pot on a medium heat, and once hot, add coconut oil (or water), shallot, garlic, ginger and sauté for 3 minutes, stirring frequently.
5. Add curry paste and cook for 2 minutes, stirring occasionally.
6. Then add coconut milk, sea salt, turmeric, maple syrup, coconut aminos, whisk to combine, and once bubbling, reduce the heat to low and simmer for 10 minutes more minutes.
7. Add lime juice, taste and adjust the flavors as needed.
8. To serve, divide the sauce between serving bowls and rest some veggies in the center along with a spoonful of (optional) rice or grain of choice. Garnish with cilantro or lime wedges (optional).

Nutritional info (per serving): 417 calories; 22.8 g fat; 45.5 g carbohydrate; 8 g protein

Vegan Pizza

Cooking time: 20 minutes   **Servings**: 2

Ingredients:

- 1/2 of garlic-herb pizza crust
- 1/2 cup each red, green, and orange bell pepper, loosely chopped
- 1/3 cup red onion, chopped
- 1 cup button mushrooms, chopped
- 1/2 teaspoon each dried or fresh basil, oregano, and garlic powder
- 1/4 teaspoon sea salt

- 1 can (15-oz) tomato sauce
- 1/2 teaspoon each dried or fresh basil, oregano, garlic powder, granulated sugar
- 1/4 teaspoon sea salt
- 1/2 cup vegan parmesan cheese
- red pepper flakes
- dried oregano

Instructions:

1. Put a rack into the middle of the oven.
2. Heat a large skillet on a medium heat, and once hot add 1 tablespoon olive oil, onion and peppers. Season with salt, herbs and stir, and cook for 10-15 minutes until soft and slightly charred adding the mushrooms in the last few minutes. Once cooked, set aside.
3. Make sauce by putting tomato sauce into a mixing bowl, adding seasonings and salt to taste. Set aside.
4. Roll out the dough onto a floured surface and transfer to a parchment-lined round baking sheet. Put pizza with the parchment directly into the oven to properly crisp the crust, so any round object will do as it's not actually going into the oven.
5. Top with the desired amount of tomato sauce, a sprinkle of parmesan cheese and the sautéed veggies.

6. Use the baking sheet to gently slide the pizza directly onto the oven rack with the parchment underneath. Otherwise it will fall through.
7. Preheat the oven to 425F and bake for 17-20 minutes or until crisp and golden brown.
8. Serve with the remaining parmesan cheese, dried oregano and red pepper flake.

Nutritional info (per serving): 395 calories; 13 g fat; 59 g carbohydrate; 15 g protein

Vegan Thai Curry

Cooking time: 40 minutes   **Servings**: 3

Ingredients:

- 2 lemongrass stalks, tough outer leaves removed, core finely chopped
- 5 spring onions, chopped
- handful fresh coriander, chopped
- 8 dried kaffir lime leaves
- 2 tablespoons tamari
- 2 green chillies, deseeded
- thumb-sized piece ginger, chopped
For the curry:
- 2 aubergines, roughly chopped
- 1 red pepper, roughly chopped
- 2 tablespoons coconut oil, melted
- 1 tablespoon sesame oil
- 1.66 cup green beans, cut into thirds
- 1.26 cup vegetable stock
- 13.5 oz can coconut milk (cream only)
- 10.6 oz buckwheat noodles
- handful cashew nuts
- 4 tablespoons desiccated coconut

Instructions:

1. Heat the oven to 395F. To make curry, put aubergines, red pepper, 1 tablespoon coconut oil in a roasting tin with, and roast for 20-25 mins until they are softened.
2. To make the paste put all the ingredients into a food processor and blend until smooth.
3. Heat sesame oil and the remaining coconut oil in a frying pan or wok, then add paste and fry for 1-2 minutes, then stir in green beans and fry for another 1-2 minutes.

4. Add vegetable stock, mixing well, followed by the roasted vegetables and the solid coconut cream from the top of the can of coconut milk. Give it all a good stir, bring to the boil, then allow it to simmer for 4-5 minutes.
5. Cook the buckwheat noodles following pack instructions.
6. Add cashews and desiccated coconut to the curry. Divide drained noodles between three bowls, top with curry, squeeze over some lime juice and garnish with red chilli.

Nutritional info (per serving): 654 calories; 36 g fat; 78 g carbohydrate; 12 g protein

Lentil Lasagna

Cooking time: 1 hour 15 minutes   **Servings**: 4

Ingredients:

- 1 tablespoon olive oil
- 1 onion, chopped
- 1 carrot, chopped
- 1 celery stick, chopped
- 1 garlic clove, crushed
- 2 cans (13.5 oz) lentils, drained, rinsed
- 1 tablespoon cornflour
- 13.5 oz can chopped tomato
- 1 teaspoon mushroom ketchup
- 1 teaspoon chopped oregano (or 1 teaspoon dried)
- 1 teaspoon vegetable stock powder
- 2 cauliflower heads, broken into florets
- 2 tablespoons unsweetened soy milk
- pinch of freshly grated nutmeg
- 9 dried egg-free lasagne sheets
- Vegan cheese

Instructions:

1. Heat oil in a pan, add onion, carrot, celery, and gently cook for 10-15 minutes until soft.
2. Add garlic, cook for a few more minutes, then stir in the lentils and corn flour.
3. Add tomatoes, a canful of water, mushroom ketchup, oregano, stock powder, some seasoning and simmer for 15 minutes, stirring occasionally.
4. Cook cauliflower in a pan of boiling water for 10 minutes or until tender. Once cooked, drain, purée with the soy milk using a hand blender or a food processor. Season well and add nutmeg.

5. Heat the oven to 356F. Spread a third of the lentil mixture over the base of a ceramic baking dish, about 8 x 12 inch. Cover with a single layer of lasagne, snapping the sheets to fit. Add another third of the lentil mixture, then spread a third of the cauliflower purée on top, followed by a layer of pasta. Top with the last third of lentils and lasagna, followed by the remaining purée.
6. Cover loosely with foil and bake for 35-45 minutes, removing the foil for the final 10 minutes of cooking. Serve topped with vegan cheese.

Nutritional info (per serving): 340 calories; 8.5 g fat; 47.1 g carbohydrate; 19.6 g protein

Mushroom Stroganoff

Cooking time: 25 minutes   **Servings**: 4

Ingredients:

- 2 tablespoons olive oil
- 1/2 yellow onion, diced
- 2 garlic cloves, finely chopped
- 1 lb baby portobello mushrooms, sliced
- 1.5 cups vegetable broth
- 2 teaspoons soy sauce or tamari
- 1 teaspoon dried thyme
- 1/2 cup vegan sour cream
- 2 tablespoons whole wheat flour
- 1 lb farfalle pasta, cooked
- salt and black pepper, to taste
- fresh parsley, chopped

Instructions:

1. Heat olive oil in a pan on a medium heat. Add onion, garlic and cook for about 5 minutes until fragrant and the onion is soft.
2. Add mushrooms and cook for about 7 minutes until juices are released and become soft.
3. Add vegetable broth, soy sauce or tamari, thyme, and stir to combine. Reduce the heat to a medium-low and simmer for about 10 minutes until the liquid has reduced by a third.
4. Add vegan sour cream, flour and continue to simmer for another 3 minutes until the sauce thickens. Once done, remove from the heat.
5. Cook pasta according to package directions, until ready. Then drain, rinse and return noodles to the pot.
6. Pour the mushroom sauce over pasta and stir to coat. Season with salt and black pepper to taste.

7. Garnish with freshly chopped parsley and serve immediately.

Nutritional info (per serving): 345 calories; 6 g fat; 60 g carbohydrate; 13 g protein

Chipotle Tofu Chilaquiles

Cooking time: 20 minutes   **Servings**: 4

Ingredients:

- 10 yellow corn tortillas
- 1 white onion, diced
- 4 garlic cloves, minced
- 2 cans (15 oz) crushed tomatoes
- 1 tablespoon avocado oil
- 2 canned chipotle in adobo sauce
- 2 tablespoons adobo sauce
- 1 cup vegetable stock
- 16 oz extra-firm tofu, drained and pressed
- 1 teaspoon cumin
- 1 teaspoon garlic powder
- ½ teaspoon chili powder
- Salsa or hot sauce, for serving
- Lime juice, for serving
- Salt, to taste

Instructions:

1. Preheat the oven to 350F.
2. Preheat oil in a large skillet over medium heat. Add onion and garlic, cook for 2-3 minutes.
3. Add tomato sauce, diced chipotle, adobo sauce, and vegetable stock. Bring to a boil and reduce the heat to low. Cook for about 5 minutes. Transfer the sauce to a blender and process until smooth.
4. Crumble the tofu with a fork and add it to the same skillet where the sauce was. Add more oil of needed and cook for 3-4 minutes. Add chili powder, garlic powder, cumin and salt. Cook for 2 minutes more. Remove from heat.
5. Add tortillas to the pan and pour the sauce on top, stir well to coat.
6. Serve topped with salsa and lime juice.

Nutritional info (per serving): 282 calories; 6.9 g fat; 44 g carbohydrate; 16.4 g protein

Mushroom Bolognese

Cooking time: 45 minutes

Servings: 4

Ingredients:

- 2 cans (28 oz each) San Marzano Tomatoes
- 1 large eggplant (or 2 smaller ones)
- 5 red bell peppers
- 3/4 lb mushrooms (your choice)
- 1 onion, diced
- 6 cloves garlic, minced
- 2 tablespoons dry oregano
- 2 tablespoons smoked paprika
- 2 leaves bay
- 1 pinch red pepper flakes
- 1/2 cup red wine (optional)
- 1 teaspoon sea salt
- 2 sprigs fresh basil, for garnish
- 2 tablespoons fresh oregano leaves
- 2 tablespoons fresh Italian parsley, chopped
- 2 lbs rigatoni or bucatini pasta

Instructions:

1. Preheat a large cast iron plate, then put eggplant, bell peppers and roast until charred all over. Once cooked, transfer to a bowl, cover with plastic wrap and allow to cool.
2. Once cool enough, remove charred skins, scoop flesh from the eggplant into a bowl and put into a food processor. Process until a nice chunky rustic texture is achieved.
3. Peel bell peppers, put into a food processor and purée until a rustic texture if formed. Refrigerate until needed.
4. Rinse and slice mushrooms if needed, depending on the variety.
5. Put olive oil, onion into a large pot and heat it on a medium flame. Give it a good stir, add mushrooms with a good pinch of sea salt. Cook until moisture is almost all reduced.
6. Add grated garlic, paprika and cook for another 10 seconds, taking good care make sure not to burn it.

7. Add oregano and red pepper flakes. (At this point you and reserve some of the mushrooms for garnish If you like)
8. Add red wine, stir well and simmer for about 5 minutes until reduced by half.
9. Add roasted eggplant, bell peppers and bay leaf to the pot and bring to a simmer.
10. Use your hands to crush tomatoes while leaving some rustic chunks for texture.
11. Stir and bring to a gentle simmer. Partially cover with a lid and cook for about 45minutes to 1 hour until the sauce had reduced to your liking.
12. Bring a large pot of water to a boil, add a good amount of sea salt. (water should taste like sea water).
13. Add Rigatoni and cook according to the directions on the box.
14. Drain the pasta and toss with the sauce. Serve with fresh herbs and reserved Mushrooms on top.

Nutritional info (per serving): 567 calories; 9 g fat; 92 g carbohydrate; 19 g protein

Broccoli Leek Casserole

Cooking time: 40 minutes   **Servings**: 4

Ingredients:

- 1/2 head medium broccoli or 3.5 cups broccoli florets
- 3 cups chopped leeks (about 2 leeks), white and light green parts only, cleaned

For the garlic cashew sauce:

- 1 cup raw cashews (soaked for at least 4 hours)
- 2 cloves garlic
- 2 cups water
- 2/3 cup nutritional yeast
- 3/4 teaspoon salt
- 1/2 teaspoon pepper (optional or more fresh cracked pepper)
- 1/4 teaspoon paprika
- 1/4 teaspoon cayenne pepper
- fresh parsley, chopped

Instructions:

1. Preheat the oven to 390F.
2. Chop broccoli into florets and steam in a steamer for 5-7 minutes until broccoli is tender. Alternatively, broccoli can be boiled in a pot for 5-7 minutes.
3. Toss broccoli and leeks together and put into a small 2-quart casserole dish.
4. Blend all sauce ingredients for the sauce in a food processor or a blender until smooth.
5. Pour sauce over broccoli and leeks until well covered.
6. Put casserole dish into an oven and bake for 40 minutes until sauce thickens and leeks soften and wilt.

7. Once cooked, remove the casserole dish from the oven. Sprinkle with paprika, cayenne pepper and chopped fresh parsley, if desired.
8. Allow casserole to cool for 5-10 minutes before eating.

Nutritional info (per serving): 343 calories; 17.7 g fat; 35.2 g carbohydrate; 19.3 g protein

Pumpkin Pasta with Spinach and Mushrooms

Cooking time: 25 minutes   **Servings**: 4

Ingredients:

- 1/2 small to medium-sized Hokkaido pumpkin
- 2 teaspoons olive oil, divided
- salt and freshly ground black pepper, to taste
- 1 head garlic
- 12 oz whole wheat pasta
- 7 oz mushrooms, sliced
- 5 oz raw spinach
- 1 cup vegetable broth
- 1 teaspoon dried basil
- 1/2 teaspoon dried sage
- 1/4 teaspoon nutmeg
- 4 tablespoons chopped walnuts, to serve
- 4 teaspoons pumpkin oil, to serve (optional)

Instructions:

1. Lay a baking tray with parchment paper and drizzle it with olive oil or cooking spray.
2. Chop pumpkin into small chunks, put pumpkin into the tray and sprinkle with salt and pepper.
3. Cut a top off a garlic head and put it into the tray.
4. Preheat the oven to 350F and bake in the preheated oven for around 20 minutes.
5. Cook pasta according to the instructions on the package.
6. Put olive oil into a large skillet and sautée chopped mushrooms for about 3 minutes on a medium heat.
7. Add spinach and continue cooking for about 4-5 minutes until it is softened. Set aside.
8. When pumpkin is roasted, transfer it to a blender together with peeled roasted garlic and pulse until smooth, adding vegetable broth.

9. Add spices, herbs, as well as salt and pepper to taste. Combine pasta with mushrooms, spinach and pumpkin puree.
10. Serve sprinkled with chopped walnuts and drizzled with pumpkin oil.

Nutritional info (per serving): 126 calories; 14 g fat; 87 g carbohydrate; 18 g protein

Fettuccine Cauliflower Alfredo

Cooking time: 15 minutes   **Servings:** 4

Ingredients:

- 1/2 medium head cauliflower
- 1/2 small onion, finely chopped
- 2 large cloves garlic, finely chopped
- 1/4 teaspoon onion powder
- 1/2 teaspoon salt, plus more to taste if required
- good grind of black pepper, plus more to taste if required
- 2-3 tablespoons nutritional yeast
- 1/4 cup vegetable broth
- 1/4 cup & 2 tablespoons non-dairy
- 1/4 teaspoon smoked paprika or chipotle powder
- 1.5 teaspoons sweet white miso paste (optional)
- 1 tablespoon olive oil (optional)
- 4 small packages NuPasta Fettuccine or 14oz dried fettuccine (or other pasta of choice)

Instructions:

1. Cook cauliflower until fork tender. Once cooked, drain and put into a blender.
2. Gently sauté onion until transparent, then add garlic and continue cooking until it starts to turn golden. Once cooked, remove from the heat and put into a blender.
3. Put all the other ingredients into a blender (except milk and fettuccine).
4. Once cooked, drain cauliflower and put other ingredients into the blender. Then blend until completely smooth.
5. Add milk gradually as needed.

Nutritional info (per serving): 57 calories; 1.6 g fat; 8.3 g carbohydrate; 4.9 g protein

Zucchini Casserole

Cooking time: 50 minutes   **Servings**: 6

Ingredients:

- 2 eggplants
- 2 zucchinis
- 5 cloves garlic, peeled and minced
- 1 15 oz tomato sauce
- 1 batch vegan white sauce
- 1 batch vegan parmesan
- good pinch of salt and pepper

Instructions:

1. Slice eggplant and zucchinis.
2. Put some white sauce on the bottom of casserole.
3. Next put a layer of eggplant slices. Season with salt and pepper.
4. Add tomato sauce, sprinkle some vegan parmesan and put a layer of zucchini slices. Season with salt and pepper.
5. Repeat these steps until all slices are gone. Last layer should be the white sauce.
6. Sprinkle with reserved vegan parmesan on top.
7. Cover with aluminum foil and bake for around 50 minutes at 400°F.

Nutritional info (per serving): 245 calories; 13 g fat; 63 g carbohydrate; 16 g protein

Roasted Red Pepper Pasta with Black Pepper Chickpeas

Cooking time: 25 minutes

Servings: 4

Ingredients:

For the black pepper chickpeas:

- 1 teaspoon oil
- 15 oz can chickpeas, drained, washed
- 1/2 teaspoon freshly ground or coarsely crushed black pepper
- 1/4 teaspoon salt
- 1/2 teaspoon dried thyme or 1 teaspoon fresh
- 1/4 teaspoon dried rosemary
- 1/4 teaspoon dried sage
- 1/2 teaspoon garlic powder

For the roasted red pepper pasta:

- 10 oz pasta of choice
- 2 teaspoons olive oil
- 1/2 cup finely chopped onion
- 3 cloves of garlic, finely chopped
- 1.5-2 roasted red peppers
- 2 tablespoons tomato paste
- 1/2 teaspoon garlic powder
- 1/2 teaspoon ground mustard
- 1/4 teaspoon each of dried thyme oregano
- 1 tablespoon or more nutritional yeast
- salt to taste
- 1/4 teaspoon black pepper
- 1/4 teaspoon red pepper flakes
- 1/4 cup cashews soaked for 15 minutes if needed
- 1.5 cups water
- fresh basil

Instructions:

1. To make the crisp chickpeas: Add oil into a skillet and heat it on a medium heat. Add chickpeas, spices, salt, herbs; toss well and cook for 6-8 minutes until crisp on the edges stirring occasionally. Taste in between to adjust salt and pepper.
2. Put everything into a bowl with an additional 1-2 teaspoons of oil and bake at 400F for 20 minutes until crisp.
3. To make the pasta:
4. Cook the pasta according to instructions on the package.
5. Put oil into a skillet and heat it on a medium heat. Add onions, garlic and cook until translucent.
6. Put half of the cooked onion garlic mixture, ingredients from roasted red peppers to water into the blender and blend until smooth.
7. Put into the skillet and bring to a boil. At this point add some veggies (chopped small) if you like.
8. Taste and adjust salt and heat. Add more salt, a pinch of sweetener if needed.
9. Fold in cooked pasta and cook for a minute. Cover and let sit for a few minutes.
10. Serve garnished with crisp peppery chickpeas and loads of fresh basil.

Nutritional info (per serving): 463 calories; 10 g fat; 76 g carbohydrate; 17 g protein

Mexican Lasagna

Cooking time: 40 minutes   **Servings**: 8

Ingredients:

- 2 cloves garlic, minced
- 1 red onion, diced
- 1 teaspoon neutral-flavored oil
- 1 green bell pepper, diced
- 1 red bell pepper, diced
- 1 ½ cups corn or 15 oz can
- 2 cups tomatoes, diced or 2 medium tomatoes
- 1 ½ cups kidney beans or 15 oz can
- 1 teaspoon chili powder
- 1/2 teaspoon onion powder
- 1/2 teaspoon garlic powder
- 1/2 teaspoon cumin
- 1/2 teaspoon sea salt
- 1/2 teaspoon ground black pepper
- 1 1/2 cups vegetarian refried beans or 15 oz can
- 12 6 or 8 inch corn tortillas (gluten-free if necessary)
- 16 oz jar salsa
- 1/2 cup cashew cheese sauce
- 1/3 cup black olives, sliced
- 2 tablespoons cilantro, minced

Instructions:

1. Put garlic, onion into a large skillet or a nonstick pan and sauté in the oil for about 3 minutes, until onions become translucent.

2. Add peppers and continue to cook for about 5 more minutes, until soften. Once cooked, remove from the heat and put into a large bowl.
3. Add corn, kidney beans, tomatoes, and spices.
4. Lightly oil a casserole dish. Spread 1/4 of salsa over the bottom of a casserole dish. Top with 4 tortillas. You can cut them to fit the dish.
5. Spread half of refried beans over tortillas and top with half of the vegetable bean mixture.
6. Spread another 1/4 of salsa over vegetables. Place 4 more tortillas over the top and repeat the layering.
7. Preheat the oven to 400F. Top with the remaining tortillas and salsa and bake for 30 minutes or until bubbly and cooked throughout.
8. Drizzle the top with cashew cheese sauce and sprinkle with olives and cilantro.

Nutritional info (per serving): 271 calories; 11.5 g fat; 32.2 g carbohydrate; 19.6 g protein

Creamy Broccoli Cheese Soup

Cooking time: 30 minutes   **Servings**: 6-8

Ingredients:

- 1 tablespoon extra-virgin olive oil
- 1 large yellow onion, finely diced (about 1 1/2 cups)
- 1 medium shallot, minced
- 1 teaspoon smoked paprika
- 2 teaspoons sea salt, divided, plus more to taste
- freshly ground black pepper, to taste
- 4 small or 2 large heads broccoli, destemmed, and chopped into small 1/2-inch florets (1 lb florets or 5-6 cups)
- 4 cups low-sodium vegetable broth, divided
- 2 cups filtered water
- 2 cups small cauliflower florets
- 1/2 cup shelled hemp seeds
- 1/2 cup chopped roasted and peeled red peppers
- 1/2 cup nutritional yeast
- 1 tablespoon arrowroot powder
- 1 tablespoon apple cider vinegar
- 1 tablespoon fresh lemon juice
- 1 tablespoon reduced-sodium tamari

Instructions:

1. Heat olive oil in a large Dutch oven or stock pot on a medium-low heat.
2. Add onion, shallot, smoked paprika, 1 teaspoon sea salt, black pepper, and cook for 6 minutes stirring occasionally or until the onion is soft and translucent.
3. Add broccoli florets, 3 cups vegetable broth, filtered water, increase the heat to a medium-high and bring to a rapid simmer for 5 minutes. Reduce the heat to medium-low, cover, and simmer for 20 to 25 minutes or until broccoli florets are fork-tender, stirring occasionally to ensure that the broccoli is submerged.
4. Bring a medium pot of water to a boil. Put cauliflower florets into the pot and boil for 7 minutes or until very fork-tender. Strain off water.
5. Add boiled cauliflower florets, remaining 1 cup vegetable broth, hemp hearts, roasted red peppers, nutritional yeast, arrowroot powder, apple cider vinegar, and the remaining 1 teaspoon sea salt to a high-speed blender. Blend on high for 2 minutes or until completely smooth and creamy.
6. Once the broccoli florets are fork-tender, pour cauliflower "cheddar" sauce into the pot and stir to combine.
7. Increase the heat to medium and continue stirring for 3-5 minutes or until the soup begins to thicken.
8. Once the soup has thickened slightly, remove from the heat and stir in the fresh lemon juice and tamari.
9. Taste and season with more sea salt, black pepper, and smoked paprika, if desired.

Nutritional info (per serving): 249 calories; 13 g fat; 12 g carbohydrate; 13 g protein

Grilled Cheese with Smoky Tomato Soup

Cooking time: 45 minutes   **Servings**: 4

Ingredients:

For the cheese:

- 1/2 can full-fat coconut milk (6.83 fl. oz.)
- 1/2 teaspoon coconut vinegar
- 1/2 teaspoon salt
- 1 teaspoon agar powder
- 1/2 tablespoon tapioca flour
- 1 tablespoon nooch

For the soup:

- 1 tablespoon olive oil
- 1 small onion, chopped
- 4 garlic cloves, smashed
- 1/2 teaspoon dried thyme
- 1/2 teaspoon dried basil
- 1/2 teaspoon dried oregano
- few dashes liquid smoke
- 1 cup prepared crushed roma tomatoes
- 2 cups homemade stock

For the sandwich:

- 4 pieces sandwich bread
- vegan butter, softened at room temperature

Instructions:

To make the cheese
1. Combine all of cheese ingredients (except the nooch) in a small saucepan.
2. Whisk briskly continuously until the mixture comes to a boil.

3. Remove it from the heat, stir in nooch and transfer it to a small pyrex dish.
4. Cover and chill in the refrigerator for at least 1 hour.
To make the soup
5. Heat oil in a medium-sized saucepan on a medium heat, add onions and sauté for about 7 minutes until translucent and slightly browned.
6. Reduce the heat to a medium low, add garlic, spices, liquid smoke and allow to sauté for about 3 minutes, stirring occassionally.
7. Now add prepared roma tomatoes and vegan broth. Return the heat to medium until soup comes to a very small boil. Then dial the heat back down to low and allow to simmer for about 15 minutes.
8. At this point, you can remove soup from the heat and blend it well with an immersion blender.
To make the sandwiches
9. Put 1/2 tablespoon vegan butter into a skillet on a medium heat.
10. Spread one of the slices of bread with a thin layer of cheese, then place bread piece cheese side up on the skillet.
11. Swirl it around to ensure it gets coated well with the vegan butter.
12. Spread the other slice of bread with softened butter and put it butter side up on top.
13. Allow bread to nicely brown for about 4 minutes on one side before flipping it over with a spatula.
14. Sprinkle with a little salt on top if desired.

Nutritional info (per serving): 71 calories; 4 g fat; 7 g carbohydrate; 1 g protein

French Dip Sandwiches

Cooking time: 35 minutes   **Servings**: 2

Ingredients:

- 2 tablespoons olive oil, divided
- 1 medium onion, sliced into half rings
- 2 garlic cloves, minced
- 3 portobello mushroom caps, (about 20 oz total), cleaned and sliced into thin strips
- 1 cup vegetable broth
- 1 tablespoon soy sauce
- 1 tablespoon vegan Worcestershire sauce
- 1/2 teaspoon dried thyme
- 1/4 teaspoon liquid smoke, (optional, but highly recommended)
- 1/4 teaspoon black pepper
- 2-6 inch sandwich rolls or baguette sections sliced open
- horseradish mustard

Instructions:

1. Coat the bottom of a large skillet with 1 tablespoon oil and place over medium-low heat.
2. Add onion and toss a few times to coat with oil. Allow to cook until caramelized, for about 20 minutes, flipping occasionally.
3. Add garlic and cook for about 2 minutes more. Transfer onions and garlic to a plate.

4. Coat skillet with another tablespoon of oil and raise heat to medium. Add mushroom strips, avoid overcrowding the skillet.
5. Cook until lightly browned, for about 5 minutes. Flip and cook 5 minutes more on the opposite sides.
6. Return onions to the skillet, add broth, soy sauce, Worchestershire sauce, thyme, liquid smoke, pepper and bring to a simmer and allow to cook, stirring occasionally, until liquid is reduced by half, for about 5 minutes.
7. Slather the insides of rolls with horseradish mustard.
8. Use a slotted spoon to remove onions and mushrooms from skillet, pressing lightly to squeeze out any excess juice.
9. Divide onions and mushrooms into rolls.
10. Pour cooking liquid into a small bowl and serve with sandwiches, for dipping.

Nutritional info (per serving): 436 calories; 20 g fat; 48 g carbohydrate; 7 g protein

French Toast

Cooking time: 26 minutes   **Servings**: 4

Ingredients:

- 1 heaping tablespoon chia seeds (whole or ground into a fine meal so they're undetectable)
- 1/2 tablespoon agave nectar or maple syrup (or sub honey if not vegan)
- 1 cup unsweetened almond milk (or any non-dairy milk)
- 1/2 teaspoon ground cinnamon
- 1/2 teaspoon vanilla extract
- 4-5 slices bread (it's important to use a sturdy, rustic bread or it can turn out soggy/soft)

Instructions:

1. Combine all ingredients (except the bread) in a large, shallow bowl. Put it into a fridge for 10-20 minutes to activate.
2. Preheat the griddle to a medium heat 350F and grease with 1 tablespoon vegan butter or coconut oil.
3. Dip each bread slice in batter for about 20 seconds on each side. If bread is dry, leave it for a little longer. If you're using sandwich bread, it should only need 25-30 seconds total to soak.
4. Put bread pieces on a griddle and cook until golden brown on the underside. Then carefully flip and cook for 3-4 minutes until the other side is golden brown.
5. Top with the desired toppings and serve.

Nutritional info (per serving): 197 calories; 6.8 g fat; 27.4 g carbohydrate; 6.2 g protein

Chickpea Flour Omelette

Cooking time: 20 minutes　　　　　**Servings**: 4

Ingredients:

- 4 tablespoons flaxmeal
- 4 tablespoons oat flour (or omit)
- 1.33 cups chickpea flour besan
- 2 cups water
- 1 teaspoon salt
- generous pinch of black salt
- generous pinch of garlic powder
- pinch of turmeric
- 2 teaspoons baking powder
- few tablespoons each: chopped onion, bell peppers, tomato, carrots(1/3-1/2 cup total veggies)
- 2 jalapeno or serano chili pepper, finely chopped (or use black pepper/cayenne to taste)
- 1 cup packed chopped spinach or greens

Instructions:

1. Put flaxmeal, warm 1/4 cup water into a bowl, whisk and let sit for 5 minutes.
2. Combine baking powder, chickpea flour. Then add oat flour, salt, spices and 1/4 cup more water and mix for half a minute to combine well and to help the batter get airy.
3. Add vegetables, jalapeno, greens and fold in well.
4. Heat a non stick pan at a medium heat and grease a little.
5. Drop batter on the hot pan and tap once or twice to spread (or use a spatula). Cover with a lid and cook for 7 minutes. Once cooked, take the lid off, add few drops of oil onto the

edges, and cook for another 5-7 minutes (depends on the consistency of the batter). Then flip and cook for another 5-6 minutes.
6. Add more greens and/or non dairy cheese, fold and serve with ketchup, toasts and hash browns.

Nutritional info (per serving): 215 calories; 7 g fat; 41 g carbohydrate; 16 g protein

Tofu Benedict with Avocado

Cooking time: 20 minutes**Servings**: 4

Ingredients:

For the tofu benedict:

- 2 English muffins
- 1 large tomato, cut into slices
- 8 oz firm tofu
- 2 tablespoons avocado oil
- salt and pepper
- 1-2 teaspoons nutritional yeast
- small handful of mixed greens
- 1 small avocado

For the vegan Hollandaise sauce:

- 2 tablespoons vegan butter
- 1 tablespoon all-purpose flour
- 1/2 cup unsweetened non-dairy milk
- 4 teaspoons nutritional yeast
- 2 teaspoons lemon juice, to taste
- salt and pepper
- pinch of cayenne

Instructions:

1. Put vegan butter into a small saucepan and bring to a boil.
2. Add flour and whisk until it forms a paste, slowly add milk, whisking continuously until well combined.

3. Bring sauce to a boil for about 1-2 minutes, whisking frequently, until sauce begins to thicken.
4. Once cooked, remove from the heat, add nutritional yeast, lemon juice, and seasoning. Stir together and set aside.
5. Slice tofu 1/2 inch thick and sprinkle each side with nutritional yeast, salt, and pepper.
6. Heat avocado oil in a cast iron skillet on a medium heat, put tofu into a pan with hot oil and pan fry on each side for about 4-5 minutes, until browned. Once cooked, remove from the heat.
7. Slice English muffins in half and toast.
8. Top each muffin with a small amount of mixed greens and one tomato slice.
9. Put pan-fried tofu atop each tomato and smother with Hollandaise Sauce.
10. Finish with sliced avocado and serve immediately.

Nutritional info (per serving): 478 calories; 35 g fat; 30 g carbohydrate; 13 g protein

Pumpkin Chili

Cooking time: 20 minutes **Servings**: 4

Ingredients:

- 2 tablespoons extra virgin olive oil
- 1 onion, finely chopped
- 1 teaspoon salt
- 1 green pepper, cored and finely chopped
- 3 cloves garlic, minced
- 2 tablespoons tomato paste
- 1 tablespoon chili powder
- 1 tablespoon cumin
- 1 teaspoon smoked paprika
- 1 teaspoon oregano
- 1 (15-oz) can pumpkin puree
- 1 (15-oz) can pinto beans, drained
- 1 (15-oz) can black beans, drained
- 1 (15-oz) can diced tomatoes with their juices
- 1 cup frozen corn kernels
- 1/2 cup vegetable broth
- avocado, sour cream, cilantro and green onion, for topping

Instructions:

1. Warm olive oil in a large deep pot on a medium heat.
2. Add onion, 1 teaspoon salt and cook for about 3 minutes until translucent.
3. Add pepper, garlic and continue cooking for 2 more minutes.
4. Next add spices, tomato paste, Stir together and cook for 2 minutes.
5. Add pumpkin puree, diced tomatoes, drained beans, corn, vegetable broth and bring to a low boil and cook for about 10 minutes until heated through.
6. Serve warm with favorite toppings.

Nutritional info (per serving): 196 calories; 7 g fat; 38 g carbohydrate; 11 g protein

Vegan Meatloaf

Cooking time: 50 minutes   **Servings**: 8

Ingredients:

For the meatloaf:

- 1 cup canned or cooked chickpeas, drained and rinsed
- 1 cup canned or cooked kidney beans, drained and rinsed
- 1 cup ground flaxseed
- 1 cup nutritional yeast
- 1/2 cup tahini
- 1/4 cup tamari or soy sauce
- 1/4 cup unsweetened plant milk of your choice
- 2 teaspoons onion powder
- 2 teaspoons garlic powder
- 1/4 teaspoon ground black pepper

For the glaze:

- 1/2 cup ketchup
- 2 tablespoons cane, coconut or brown sugar
- 1 teaspoon onion powder
- 1 teaspoon garlic powder
- 1/2 teaspoon paprika

Instructions:

1. Put chickpeas, beans into a mixing bowl and mash with a fork or a potato masher.
2. Add the rest of the meatloaf ingredients and mix until well combined (you can also blend all the ingredients in a food processor).

3. Press the mixture firmly in a lined 9×5-inch loaf pan (feel free to place the mixture onto a lined baking sheet and form it into a loaf pan with your hands).
4. In order to make the glaze just mix all the ingredients in a mixing bowl until well combined
5. Preheat the oven to 350F. Spread the glaze evenly over the top and bake for 50 minutes.
6. Once cooked, remove from the oven and allow vegan meatloaf to cool for at least 5 minutes before removing it from the loaf pan.

Nutritional info (per serving): 172 calories; 6 g fat; 21 g carbohydrate; 10 g protein

Baked Squash

Cooking time: 2 hours 30 minutes   **Servings:** 4

Ingredients:

- 1 butternut squash
- olive oil
- 1 red onion
- 1 clove garlic
- 1 bunch fresh sage
- 10 sun-dried tomatoes
- 2.65 oz packed chestnuts or pecans
- 2.65 oz basmati rice
- 2.65 oz dried cranberries
- 1 pinch ground allspice
- red wine

Instructions:

1. Wash the squash, carefully cut it in half lengthways, remove and reserve the seeds. Use a spoon to score and scoop some flesh out, making a gully for the stuffing all along the length of the squash.
2. Finely chop the scooped-out flesh, put into a frying pan and fry on a medium heat with 2 tablespoons of oil.
3. Peel, finely chop and add onion, garlic, and stir regularly while you pick sage leaves and finely chop them with the sun-dried tomatoes and chestnuts.
4. Put into the pan with rice, cranberries and allspice; add a good pinch of sea salt and black pepper and a swig of red wine, mix well. Fry for 10 minutes, stirring occasionally, or until softened.
5. Pack the mixture tightly into the gully in two squash halves, then press halves firmly back together.

6. Rub the squash skin with a little oil, salt, pepper, and if you've got them, pat on any extra herb leaves you have to hand.
7. Put squash into the centre of a double layer of tin foil, tightly wrap it up.
8. Preheat the oven to 350F and bake for around 2 hours, or until soft and cooked through.
9. Once ready, take squash to the table, carve into nice thick slices and serve with all the usual trimmings.

Nutritional info (per serving): 245 calories; 5.1 g fat; 46.2 g carbohydrate; 5.8 g protein

Caesar Salad

Cooking time: 2 hours 30 minutes   **Servings**: 4

Ingredients:

- 1 cup raw cashews
- 1 cup non-dairy milk
- 2 tablespoons lemon juice
- 3 cloves garlic
- 2 teaspoons Dijon mustard
- 5 kalamata olives
- salt & pepper to taste
- romaine lettuce
- 3 slices whole-grain bread
- handful croutons

Instructions:

1. Soak cashews for at least 4 hours (the longer you soak them, the easier it will be to blend into the final dressing). Once soaked, drain the soaking liquid.
2. Combine all ingredients (except lettuce and bread in a high-powered blender or a food processor, and blend for couple of minutes, until cashews to turn into a creamy sauce with no chunks remaining.
3. If the mixture is too thick, slowly add several tablespoons water at a time and continue blending until it has the perfect salad dressing consistency. Adjust the seasoning.
4. Cover and refrigerate (cashew sauces tend to get much better after chilling for several hours. It can be saved (sealed) for several days in the refrigerator).
5. When ready to serve, chop the romaine lettuce and put it into a large bowl with as much dressing as you'd like. Toss and evenly coat the lettuce.
6. Garnish with homemade whole wheat croutons (below).

Nutritional info (per serving): 543 calories; 29.9 g fat; 57.4 g carbohydrate; 23 g protein

Vegan Cobb Salad

Cooking time: 2 hours 30 minutes　　　**Servings**: 4

Ingredients:

- 6 cups chopped fresh spinach (or another salad green for the base)
- 1 cup mandarin oranges, drained
- 1/3 cup sliced black olives
- 1/2 cup chopped sweet onion, tossed in black pepper
- 1 avocado, chopped, tossed in the juice of 1 large lemon
- 1 cup cherry tomatoes, halved
- 3/4 cup tempeh bacon bits
- 1 cup chilled kidney beans, drained
- 1 cup palm hearts, diced, tossed in 1/8 teaspoon turmeric + 1 teaspoon olive oil + 1 tablespoon apple cider vinegar + 1 tablespoon nutritional yeast

Instructions:

1. Toss spinach in a light salad dressing (only if serving immediately).
2. Toss half palm heats in a yellow turmeric mix.
3. Continue assembling salad by adding all ingredients in thin rows across the top.
4. Once done, it is ready to serve.

Nutritional info (per serving): 268 calories; 19 g fat; 21 g carbohydrate; 8 g protein

Veggie Dogs

Cooking time: 30 minutes   **Servings**: 6

Ingredients:

- ½ medium onion, coarsely chopped
- 3 cloves garlic
- 3/4 cup cooked pinto beans, well-drained
- 1/2 cup plus 2 tablespoons water
- 2 tablespoons coconut aminos or soy sauce
- 1 tablespoon tomato paste
- 2 teaspoons smoked paprika
- 1 teaspoon ground coriander
- 1 teaspoon ground mustard
- 1/2 teaspoon white or black pepper
- 1/4 teaspoon celery seed
- 1/4 teaspoon mace
- 1/8 teaspoon hickory smoked salt (optional but good)
- 1 cup vital wheat gluten
- 1/3 cup oatmeal rolled or quick oats, uncooked
- 2 tablespoons nutritional yeast
- 1 tablespoon ground flax seeds

Instructions:

1. Put onion, garlic into a food processor and pulse to chop finely.
2. Heat a small non-stick skillet. Add onion, garlic and cook until onion is softened, for about 3 minutes. Transfer onion mixture back to a food processor.
3. Add pinto beans, water, coconut aminos or soy sauce, tomato paste, all seasonings to the food processor and blend until it's a thin paste.
4. Combine the remaining ingredients (gluten, oatmeal, yeast, and flax) in a large mixing bowl.
5. Add contents of the food processor and stir until combined (if it seems that there's not enough moisture, add another tablespoon or two of water).

6. Knead in a bowl for about 2 minutes until a heavy gluten dough is formed.
7. Put steamer into a pot of water and bring the water to a boil.
8. Cut off 8 pieces of aluminum foil or parchment paper, each about 6 inches long and divide the gluten into 8 equal pieces. Place a piece of foil or parchment on the counter.
9. Roll a piece of gluten between the palms of your hands until it's about the size and shape of a hot dog, and place it on the foil/paper and roll up.
10. Roll the tube back and forth, pressing lightly with your hands, to give it an even shape, and then twist the ends closed.
11. Repeat with the remaining gluten to form 8 veggie hot dogs.
12. Put all veggie dogs on the top of a steamer, cover, and steam for 45 minutes. Remove from heat and allow to cool slightly before unwrapping.
13. Store veggie dogs in a covered container in a refrigerator. Warm gently in a frying pan or a microwave or on a grill before serving.

Nutritional info (per serving): 136 calories; 1.5 g fat; 23.1 g carbohydrate; 8.4 g protein

Eggplant Parmesan with Cashew Ricotta

Cooking time: 1 hour 45 minutes   **Servings**: 4

Ingredients:

- 3 tablespoons olive oil
- 1/2 medium onion
- 2 garlic cloves, minced
- 1 (28 oz) can crushed or diced tomatoes
- 2 large eggplants
- salt
- fresh ground pepper
- 1 teaspoon dried oregano, or 1 tablespoon minced fresh oregano
- 2 tablespoons minced fresh flat-leaf parsley
- 1 bunch fresh basil, stemmed and leaves torn into large pieces
- 1 cashew ricotta
- 1 cup dried bread crumbs
- 1/2 cup non-flavored, non-dairy milk

For the cashew ricotta:

- 3/4 cup raw cashew pieces (4 oz)
- 2 tablespoons fresh lemon juice
- 1 garlic clove
- 1 tablespoon extra-virgin olive oil
- 8 oz extra-firm tofu, drained
- 1/2 teaspoon salt
- 2 grinds black pepper

Instructions:

To make the cashew ricotta:

1. In a food processor, combine cashews, 2 tablespoons lemon juice, 1 garlic clove, 1 tablespoon extra virgin olive oil, tofu, 1/2 teaspoon salt and 2 grinds of pepper.
2. Process until smooth and creamy, for 2-3 minutes. Set aside.

To make the eggplant:

3. In a large skillet, heat 1 tablespoon olive oil on a medium heat.
4. Add onion and saute until soft and translucent for about 4-5 minutes. Add garlic and saute for 1 minute.
5. Add tomatoes, their juices and cook, stirring occasionally until thick, for 25-30 minutes.
6. Let cool, then transfer to a blender or a food processor and blend until smooth.
7. Heat the oven to 400F.
8. Coat an 8 inch square baking pan with a little olive oil.
9. Trim the ends of the eggplants, then cut eggplants lengthwise into 1/4 inch thick slices.
10. Put non-dairy milk into a bowl and bread crumbs on a plate.
11. Dip each slice into non-dairy milk and then into bread crumbs until each slice is coated lightly in the crumbs.
12. In a large skillet, heat a tablespoon of olive oil on a medium-high heat.
13. Put as many eggplant slices as fit in the skillet and cook until golden brown, turning once, for 2 to 3 minutes per side.
14. Transfer to paper towels to drain, then season lightly with salt and pepper. Repeat with the remaining eggplant.
15. Stir oregano and 1 tablespoon of parsley into the cashew ricotta.
16. Spread one-fourth of tomato sauce on the bottom of the prepared pan, then arrange one-third of eggplant slices on top of the sauce.
17. Sprinkle one-third of basil leaves over the eggplant.
18. Spread one-third of cashew ricotta (about ½ cup) evenly over the basil leaves.
19. Repeat the layers two more times: sauce, eggplant, basil and cashew ricotta.
20. Spread the remaining sauce over the last layer of cashew ricotta.
21. If you have some extra bread-crumbs, you can also sprinkle bread crumbs over the top to give it a crunchy top.
22. Bake for 45 to 60 minutes, until the juices are bubbling. Let stand for 10 minutes before cutting and serving.

Nutritional info (per serving): 530 calories; 31.6 g fat; 52.5 g carbohydrate; 17.6 g protein

Lasagna with Basil Cashew Cheese

Cooking time: 1 hour   **Servings**: 6

Ingredients:

For the cheese:

- 1 cup raw cashews, soaked in water for 30 minutes or overnight
- 2 garlic cloves, peeled
- 1/4 cup fresh lemon juice
- 1 tablespoon Dijon mustard
- 1/4 cup vegetable broth or water (or more as needed)
- 1.5 cups fresh basil leaves (lightly packed)
- 1/2 cup nutritional yeast (gives the cheese flavour)
- 3/4-1 teaspoon kosher salt (or to taste) + freshly ground black pepper
- 1/2 teaspoon onion powder (optional)

For the lasagna:

- 1 lb box of lasagna noodles
- 1.5 bottles of pasta sauce or use homemade marinara sauce
- 3 garlic cloves, minced
- 1 sweet onion (2.5 cups), chopped
- 2 small zucchini, chopped
- 1 cup cremini mushrooms, sliced
- 1 large red pepper, chopped
- 1 large handful spinach
- 2 pre-cooked veggie burgers, crumbled (optional)
- lemon basil cheese sauce (from above)
- daiya cheese (as much as desired)

Instructions:

1. Drain and rinse soaked cashews. With the food processor turned on, drop in your garlic cloves and process until chopped. Add in the rest of the ingredients and process until smooth, scraping down the bowl as needed.
2. In a large skillet, sauté onion and garlic on a low-medium heat for 5 minutes. Now add the rest of veggies and sauté for another 10-15 minutes. Season well with Herbamare or kosher salt and black pepper.
3. Bring a large pot of water to boil. Boil lasagna noodles for 8 minutes, drain, and rinse immediately with cold water.
4. Add 1 cup pasta sauce on the bottom of your casserole dish. Add a layer of noodles, half of basil cheese sauce, half of vegetables, more pasta sauce, another layer of noodles, veggie burger crumbles (optional), the rest of cheese sauce, the rest of the vegetables, more pasta sauce, and finally a sprinkle of cheese.
5. Preheat the oven to 400F. Cover with tinfoil and prick with fork a few times. Bake at 400F for 40-45 minutes and then remove tinfoil and broil for 5 minutes on medium. Watch closely so you don't burn the edges.

Nutritional info (per serving): 436 calories; 21.5 g fat; 32.4 g carbohydrate; 23 g protein

Lentil Steaks with Mushroom Gravy

Cooking time: 20 minutes   **Servings:** 4

Ingredients:

- 2 cups lentils, cooked
- ½ cup vegetable broth + 2 cups broth for gravy
- ¼ cup soy sauce
- 1 cup vital wheat gluten
- 1 cup bread crumbs
- ¼ cup liquid smoke
- 2 tablespoons olive oil
- 8 oz mushrooms, sliced
- 3 tablespoons flour
- 2 garlic cloves, minced
- 3 tablespoons vegan butter
- ½ teaspoon dried oregano
- ½ teaspoon dried thyme
- Salt, pepper, to taste

Instructions:

1. Mash cooked lentils with a masher or a fork, in a large bowl. Add wheat gluten, breadcrumbs, ½ cup vegetable broth, soy sauce, liquid smoke, salt and pepper, mix well. Continue to mix with your hands until well combined. Knead for a few minutes until the mixture forms a dough ball.
2. Separate big balls from the dough and flatter to form steaks.
3. Heat 1 tablespoon oil in a pan over medium heat. Cook steaks for 2-3 minutes on each side. Set cooked steaks aside.
4. Heat 1 more tablespoon oil in a pan. Add mushrooms and garlic. Sauté for 2-3 minutes, add salt and pepper, cook until mushrooms are soft and brown.
5. Reduce heat to low, add flour and butter. Stir for some time, add 2 cups broth. Bring to a boil and let simmer for 2-4 minutes.

6. Serve steaks topped with gravy.

Nutritional info (per serving): 354 calories; 11.5 g fat; 33.6 g carbohydrate; 13 g protein

Vegan Carbonara

Cooking time: 10 minutes   **Servings:** 4

Ingredients:

- 12 oz spaghetti, uncooked
- 1 tablespoon oil
- 1 onion, chopped
- 2 garlic cloves, minced
- 2 ½ cup almond milk
- ¼ cup flour
- 1 tablespoon nutritional yeast
- 2 teaspoons soy sauce
- ½ cup sundried tomatoes, dry, sliced
- ¼ teaspoon liquid smoke
- Salt, black pepper, to taste

Instructions:

1. Bring a large sauce pan of water to a boil. Add pasta and cook for 8-10 minutes or according to the package instructions.
2. Mix sundried tomatoes, liquid smoke and soy sauce in a bowl and let rest, set aside while you cook the sauce.
3. Preheat oil in a large pan over medium heat. Add onion and garlic, cook for 4-5 minutes.
4. Add flour, whisk for 1 minute and add milk, nutritional yeast, salt and pepper. Cook for 5 minutes. Add more milk if the sauce is too thick.
5. Add sauce and marinated sundried tomatoes to cooked pasta and mix well. Serve and enjoy!

Nutritional info (per serving): 551 calories; 8 g fat; 97 g carbohydrate; 21 g protein

Vegan Tortilla Soup

Cooking time: 20 minutes   **Servings**: 4

Ingredients:

- 1 can (14 oz) black beans, rinsed and drained
- 1 can (14 oz) hominy, rinsed and drained
- 1 can (14 oz) crushed tomatoes
- 1 dried smoked chili pepper
- 1 tablespoon olive oil
- 1 white onion, diced
- 2 garlic cloves, minced.
- 1 medium jalapeños, deseeded and chopped
- 1 teaspoon ground cumin
- 4 cups vegetable stock
- 6 corn tortillas, sliced into strips
- 1 avocado, diced
- 2 radishes, sliced
- 1 handful cilantro leaves, chopped
- 1 lime, cut into wedges
- Salt, pepper, to taste

Instructions:

1. Preheat the oven to 475 F.
2. Coat a baking sheet with oil. Coat the tortilla strips with oil and arrange them in a single layer. Bake for 6-8 minutes. Season with salt and set aside.
3. Place the dried chili pepper onto a baking sheet and bake for about 1 minute. Open the pepper and remove seeds when cooled down.
4. Preheat some oil in a medium pan over medium heat. Add onion, garlic and jalapeno, cook for 4-5 minutes.

5. Add cumin, tomatoes and vegetable stock. Cook for 3 minutes, add hominy, black beans and toasted chili peppers. Cook for 8-10 minutes. Season with salt and pepper to taste.
6. Once cooked, discard the dried chili pepper. Divide avocado, radishes and tortilla strip among bowls. Top with soup, cilantro leaves and lime wedges.

Nutritional info (per serving): 182 calories; 12 g fat; 17 g carbohydrate; 2 g protein

Mushroom Bean Avocado Toast

Cooking time: 5 minutes   **Servings**: 2

Ingredients:

- 1 avocado, mashed
- 1 tablespoon (14 ml) lemon juice
- 1 tablespoon (14 ml) oil
- 4 oz (113 g) mushrooms
- ½ cup (64 g) cooked cannellini beans
- 1 oz (28 g) microgreens
- 1 tablespoon (14 g) miso paste
- 1 tablespoon (14 ml) balsamic vinegar
- 4 slices whole grain bread, toasted
- 1 tablespoon (14 g) sesame seeds, for serving

Instructions:

1. Mix avocado and lemon juice in a bowl. Set aside.
2. Preheat oil in a pan over medium heat. Add mushrooms and cook for 5 minutes. Add beans and microgreens and turn off the heat.
3. Mix miso paste and 1 tablespoon water in a bowl. Add to mushrooms and beans, mix to combine. Add vinegar and set aside.
4. Spread avocado on each bread slice. Spoon mushroom mixture on top. Top with sesame seeds and serve.

Nutritional info (per serving): 581 calories; 29.5 g fat; 65.6 g carbohydrate; 21.6 g protein

Roasted Cauliflowers with Tomato Sauce

Cooking time: 30 minutes   **Servings**: 4

Ingredients:

- 1 tablespoon olive oil
- 1 onion, chopped
- 2 carrots, chopped
- 1 cup mushrooms, chopped
- 2 cups tomato sauce
- 1 tablespoon vegan Worcestershire sauce
- 4 small whole cauliflowers
- ½ cup baby spinach
- ½ cup vegan cheese, shredded

Instructions:

1. Put olive oil into a sauté pan and heat it. Then add onion, carrot and mushrooms and cook for 10 minutes.
2. Add tomato paste and vegan Worcestershire sauce, and simmer for 10 minutes.
3. Put cauliflowers into the microwave and cook for about 5 minutes to soften.
4. Put spinach on the bottom of an ovenproof dish. Top with cauliflowers and pour over the vegetable sauce.
5. Preheat the oven to 375F, cover with foil and bake for 10 minutes. Later top with vegand cheese, put back into the oven for 5 minutes to melt the cheese.

Nutritional info (per serving): 407 calories; 22 g fat; 9 g carbohydrate; 19 g protein

Tofu Cashew Coconut Curry

Cooking time: 30 minutes   **Servings**: 4

Ingredients:

- 1 package extra firm tofu, drained, cubed
- 1 sweet potato, diced
- ½ cauliflower head, broken into florets, chopped
- 1 jalapeño, diced
- 1 bell pepper, diced
- 2 carrots, chopped
- 3 garlic cloves, minced
- 1 tablespoon virgin coconut oil
- 1 tablespoon fresh ginger, grated
- 2 tablespoons curry powder
- ½ teaspoon turmeric
- ½ teaspoon cumin
- ¼ teaspoon ground cinnamon
- 1 can (14 oz) light coconut milk
- 1 cup tomato sauce
- 1 cup vegetarian broth
- 3 tablespoons roasted cashews, ground
- Salt, to taste
- Fresh cilantro, chopped, for serving

Instructions:

1. Preheat oil in a pot over medium heat. Add garlic, ginger, potato, jalapeno, bell pepper, carrots and cauliflower. Cook for 10 minutes stirring often.
2. Add curry powder, turmeric, cumin, cinnamon and salt. Add coconut milk, tomato sauce, broth and cashews. Stir well until combined.
3. Add tofu, stir once again. Cook on low heat for 20 minutes. Serve topped with cilantro.

Nutritional info (per serving): 342 calories; 20.4 g fat; 26.2 g carbohydrate; 14.1 g protein

Vegan Frittata

Cooking time: 45 minutes **Servings:** 6

Ingredients:

- 1 ½ cup chickpea flour
- 1 ½ cup water
- ¼ cup plain vegan yogurt
- 1 tablespoon oil
- ½ cup fresh cilantro, chopped
- ½ teaspoon ground turmeric
- ¼ teaspoon dried thyme
- 2 cups broccoli flowers, chopped
- 1 onion, chopped
- ½ cup frozen peas
- Salt, pepper, to taste

Instructions:

1. Mix flour, water, yogurt, oil, turmeric, thyme and salt in a bowl or use a blender to mix well.
2. Preheat oven to 375F. Line a baking dish (9 inch) with a parchment paper.
3. Add broccoli, onion, peas and cilantro to frittata batter and pour it all into a baking dish. Cook for 45-50 minutes. Let cool a little before serving.

Nutritional info (per serving): 211 calories; 10.6 g fat; 23.8 g carbohydrate; 7.7 g protein

Spinach Ravioli

Cooking time: 10 minutes   **Servings:** 4

Ingredients:

- 1 package (12 oz) vegan wonton wrappers
- 8 oz spinach, frozen
- 1 cup vegan ricotta
- ¼ cup fresh basil, chopped
- 3-4 cups water
- Salt, pepper, to taste

Instructions:

1. Mix basil, ricotta, spinach, salt and pepper in a bowl.
2. Place wrappers on a counter. Put about 1 tablespoon filling in the center of each wrapper, put another wrapper on top and press down with your fingers to seal. Repeat with the rest of wrappers.
3. Bring water to a boil in a sauce pan. Add ravioli and cook for 2-3 minutes. Serve hot topped with some more fresh basil.

Nutritional info (per serving): 171 calories; 1.4 g fat; 23.9 g carbohydrate; 13.7 g protein

Peanut Noodles

Cooking time: 10 minutes   **Servings:** 4

Ingredients:

- ½ package rice noodles
- 3 tablespoons peanut butter
- ¼ cup soy sauce
- 3 green onions, chopped
- 1 tablespoon apple cider vinegar
- 1 tablespoon Hoisin sauce
- ¼ teaspoon ground ginger
- 1 package frozen veggies of choice
- ¼ cup water
- 2 garlic cloves, minced

Instructions:

1. Prepare a large pan. Add all the ingredients except for noodles and vegetables to a pan. Heat over medium heat until bubbly and turn off the heat, stir well.
2. Bring a medium sauce pan of water to a boil and turn off the heat. Add noodles and frozen vegetables, let stay for 10 minutes and drain.
3. Serve veggies and noodles with sauce on top.

Nutritional info (per serving): 540 calories; 26 g fat; 60 g carbohydrate; 19 g protein

Creamy Vegan Pasta

Cooking time: 18 minutes   **Servings**: 3

Ingredients:

- 1 onion, chopped
- 2 cloves garlic, minced
- 1 zucchini, chopped
- 1 small red bell pepper, chopped
- 4.5 cups uncooked fusilli
- 1.5 teaspoons red curry paste
- 3 cups diced tomatoes, canned (do not drain)
- 1 cup canned coconut milk (whole fat) (use the creamy part)
- 1/2 cup frozen peas
- 1/2 cup cherry tomatoes, cut into halves
- salt, to taste
- black pepper, to taste
- 1 teaspoon fresh lemon juice

Instructions:

1. Heat some oil in a large pot and sauté onion for about 2-3 minutes. Then add garlic, zucchini, red bell pepper and cook for 2 more minutes.
2. Add the remaining ingredients except for the cherry tomatoes. Cook for about 15 minutes uncovered and on a medium heat.
3. Then add cherry tomatoes and cook for 2 more minutes. Season with salt and black pepper.

Nutritional info (per serving): 529 calories; 19 g fat; 79 g carbohydrate; 19 g protein

Taco Pizza

Cooking time: 10 minutes   **Servings**: 3

Ingredients:

- 1 cup walnuts
- 1 cup brown lentils
- 1 tablespoon olive oil
- 1/2 onion
- 1 tablespoon tomato paste
- 1/2 cup diced tomatoes
- 1 teaspoon cumin
- 1 teaspoon paprika powder
- 2 teaspoons oregano
- salt, to taste
- black pepper, to taste
- 1 pre-made pizza dough
- 1 cup vegan sour cream
- 1 avocado, cut into pieces
- 2 tomatoes, cut into pieces
- 2 cups lettuce, cut into stripes
- 1/2 cup kidney beans
- 1/2 cup corn
- 1/2 cup vegan cheese
- red pepper flakes (optional)

Instructions:

1. Cook lentils according to the instructions. Drain and set aside.
2. In a medium pan, roast walnuts without oil for about 2 minutes or until they're lightly golden.
3. Put walnuts and cooked lentils into a food processor and process until chopped.
4. In a medium pan, heat olive oil on a medium heat and sauté onions for about 3 minutes.
5. Add lentil walnut mixture and stir in the tomato paste and cook for 2 minutes.
6. Add diced tomatoes and spices (paprika powder, cumin, oregano) and season with salt and pepper.

7. Preheat the oven to 385F and bake the pizza dough for about 10 minutes until it's golden and crispy.
8. After baking, evenly spread pizza with vegan sour cream.
9. Add a layer of vegan lentil walnut meat and top with avocado, tomatoes, lettuce, corn, kidney beans, and vegan cheese.
10. Sprinkle with red pepper flakes.

Nutritional info (per serving): 364 calories; 14 g fat; 47 g carbohydrate; 12 g protein

Vegan Chili Cheese Fries

Cooking time: 15 minutes

Servings: 2

Ingredients:

For the vegan chili:

- 1.25 cups canned kidney beans
- 1.5 cups canned black beans
- 3/4 cup canned corn
- 2 cloves of garlic, minced
- 1 onion, chopped
- 1 teaspoon paprika powder
- 1 teaspoon chili powder
- 2 tablespoons tomato paste
- 1 teaspoon cumin
- 1/4 teaspoon liquid smoke (optional)
- 1 tablespoon oregano
- salt, to taste
- black pepper, to taste
- 1 14 oz can diced tomatoes

For the fries:

- 3 large potatoes
- salt, to taste
- 1 tablespoon olive oil

For the cheese sauce:

- 1/2 cup cashews
- 1 clove of garlic
- 1 teaspoon white miso paste
- 1/2 heaped cup white beans
- 1/2 cup nutritional yeast
- 1/4 cup unsweetened plant-based milk (preferably soy, almond, or oat)
- 1/2 teaspoon paprika powder
- salt, to taste
- black pepper, to taste

Additional ingredients:

- green onions and fresh cilantro, to serve
- black olives, cut into rings
- fresh cilantro

Instructions:

1. Preheat the oven to 350F. Cut potatoes into French fries and bake for about 30 minutes until crispy.
2. Heat some oil in a large pan and sauté onion for about 2 minutes.
3. Then add garlic and cook it for 1 more minute.
4. Add the tomato paste, chili and paprika powder, and cook for 2 minutes.
5. Now add liquid smoke (if using), cumin, diced tomatoes, oregano, kidney beans, black beans, and the corn. Simmer for 10 minutes.
6. To make the vegan cheese sauce, combine all ingredients in a high speed blender and blend until smooth and creamy.
7. Once fries are ready, add chili and cheese on top and bake for another 10 minutes.
8. Serve with green onions, fresh cilantro, and black onions.

Nutritional info (per serving): 402 calories; 1.7 g fat; 88 g carbohydrate; 14.9 g protein

Saucy Meatballs with Spaghetti

Cooking time: 30 minutes

Servings: 4

Ingredients:

For the vegan meatballs:

- 1 15 oz can kidney beans
- 1/2 tablespoon olive oil
- 1 large clove of garlic, minced
- 1/2 onion, chopped
- 1 teaspoon oregano
- 1 teaspoon basil
- 1 tablespoon tomato paste
- 1 teaspoon soy sauce
- 1/2 cup rolled oats
- 1/3 heaped cup sunflower seeds
- salt
- black pepper

For the chunky marinara sauce:

- 1/2 tablespoon olive oil
- 1 small onion, chopped
- 1 large clove garlic, minced
- 1 carrot, cut into small pieces
- 1 tablespoon tomato paste
- 1/4 cup dry red wine
- 1 can diced tomatoes (14,5 oz)
- 1 teaspoon oregano
- fresh basil leaves, cut into small pieces
- salt
- black pepper
- For the spaghetti:
- 9 oz whole wheat spaghetti

For the cashew Parmesan:

- 1/2 cup unsalted cashews
- 2 tablespoons nutritional yeast
- 1/4 teaspoon garlic powder
- salt

Instructions:

1. Cook the spaghetti according to the instructions on the package.
2. Rinse and drain the kidney beans. Put them in a medium bowl and mash them well with a fork or a potato masher.
3. In a medium pan, heat some oil and sauté the onions for 3 minutes. Add the minced garlic and cook for another minute.
4. Put the sunflower seeds in a food processor and pulse until a fine meal is achieved.
5. Add the sauteed onion and garlic to the mashed beans together with the spices, the tomato paste, the soy sauce, the ground sunflower seeds, and the oats. Season with salt and pepper.
6. Use your hands to thoroughly mix everything. Then form about 12-14 vegan meatballs. (Please note that I doubled the recipe for the photos, so there are more meatballs).
7. Preheat the oven to 350F and bake the vegan meatballs for about 15 minutes. Carefully flip them halfway through the baking time.
8. Alternatively you could also pan-fry them. In a medium pan, heat some olive oil over medium heat and gently roast the bean balls for about 4 minutes until they are golden. You'll achieve the best results with a cast iron pan. However, I would recommend the baking version. Not only is this version oil-free, they meatballs also become more crispier and firmer this way.
9. Make the marinara sauce: In a medium pan, heat the olive oil over medium heat. Sauté the onions for 3 minutes, then add the garlic and the carrot. Cook for another 2-3 minutes. Stir in the tomato paste and cook for 2 minutes.
10. Then deglaze with red wine and allow to evaporate. Add diced tomatoes and simmer for about 10 minutes. Season with oregano, salt, and pepper. Before serving add some fresh basil leaves.
11. Make the cashew Parmesan: Put the cashews, nutritional yeast, salt, and garlic powder in a food processor and pulse until a fine meal is achieved.
12. Serve the spaghetti with the marinara and vegan meatballs and sprinkle with Parmesan and fresh basil leaves.

Nutritional info (per serving): 459 calories; 12 g fat; 73 g carbohydrate; 17 g protein

Chickpea Curry with Potatoes

Cooking time: 25 minutes   **Servings**: 3

Ingredients:

- Jasmine rice
- 1 small onion, cut into stripes
- 2 small potatoes, cut into small pieces
- 1 large carrot, cut into slices
- 1 teaspoon curry powder
- 1 teaspoon red curry paste (optional) adjust if the curry paste you're using is very spicy, mine was very mild
- 1 cup full fat coconut milk
- 1/2 cup vegetable broth
- 1 1/2 cups cooked chickpeas
- 1 cup frozen peas
- salt
- black pepper
- cashews (optional)
- fresh cilantro (optional)

Instructions:

1. Cook the Jasmine rice according to the instructions on the package.
2. In a large pan, heat some oil and sauté the onion for 2-3 minutes. Then add the potatoes and cook for another 3 minutes. Stir in the red curry paste and the curry and cook for another minute.
3. Add the coconut milk, vegetable broth, carrot, chickpeas, and peas and cook for about 20 minutes.
4. Season with salt and pepper and serve with cashews and cilantro.

Nutritional info (per serving): 404 calories; 21 g fat; 46 g carbohydrate; 12 g protein

Classic Vegan Coleslaw

Cooking time: 10 minutes   **Servings**: 8

Ingredients:

- 1 small head green cabbage (about 6 – 7 cups), shredded
- 1/2 small red cabbage (about 3 cups), shredded
- 1.5 cups carrots, shredded or julienned
- 2/3 cup vegan mayonnaise
- 1 tablespoon Dijon mustard
- 2 tablespoons apple cider vinegar
- 1-2 teaspoons pure cane sugar
- salt & pepper, to taste

Instructions:

1. To make the dressing, whisk the mayonnaise in a small bowl,, apple cider vinegar, mustard, sugar, salt, and pepper.
2. Put cabbage and carrots into a very large mixing bowl, the larger the better. Pour the dressing all over the cabbage, and toss well to combine.
3. Serve right away, or let the coleslaw rest in the fridge for at least 30 minutes before serving.
4. Store leftovers in the refrigerator in an airtight container for up to 5 days, but it's best within 3 days.

Nutritional info (per serving): 116 calories; 6.9 g fat; 11.6 g carbohydrate; 3.4 g protein

Herbed Potato, Asparagus and Chickpeas

Cooking time: 40 minutes   **Servings**: 3

Ingredients:

- 1 lb baby red potatoes, sliced in half lengthwise
- 1.5 cups petite baby carrots
- 1 can (14oz.) chickpeas, drained and rinsed
- 1 teaspoon of each dried basil, dried thyme, dried oregano (see notes)
- 1 teaspoon paprika
- 1/2 teaspoon garlic powder

- 2-3 tablespoons olive oil, divided
- 1 lb asparagus, ends trimmed and cut into thirds
- 1/2 large yellow onion, sliced lengthwise
- mineral salt & fresh cracked pepper, to taste
- fresh parsley, to serve

Instructions:

1. Preheat oven to 425 . Line a rimmed baking sheet with parchment paper, silpat or lightly grease with oil.
2. Add the potatoes, carrots and chickpeas to the sheet pan, drizzle with 1 1/2 tablespoon olive oil and 3/4 of the spices, toss to coat. Arrange the potatoes flesh side down, this will help them get crispy edges. Place in the oven for 20 -25 minutes.
3. Carefully remove the pan from the oven, push the potato mixture to one side, add the onion and asparagus, add the remaining oil and herb/spice mix, toss to coat. Place sheet pan back in the oven and roast for 10 – 15 minutes more.

4. Let cool a few minutes. Serve with parsley sprinkled over top and sliced avocado on the side. Would be great with a serving of quinoa on the side as well, adding more fiber and protein!
5. Store leftovers in an airtight container in the refrigerator for up to 5 – 6 days.

Nutritional info (per serving): 356 calories; 9.6 g fat; 58.6 g carbohydrate; 11.8 g protein

Banana Chia Pudding

Cooking time: 6 hours **Servings**: 4

Ingredients:

- 2 large overripe bananas
- 2 cups unsweetened coconut (beverage), almond or cashew milk
- 6 tablespoons chia seeds
  Optional add-ins:
- 2–4 tablespoons pure maple syrup
- 1/2–1 teaspoon vanilla extract
  To garnish:
- toasted coconut flakes
- banana slices
- cacao nibs or shaved dark chocolate

Instructions:

1. In a medium bowl, add bananas and mash well, stir in non-dairy milk and chia seeds, mix well.
2. Let set for about 30 minutes, and give a good stir, repeat one more time, stirring again after 30 minutes. This step is an important step, as the seeds need to be stirred once or twice before completely gelling up and setting. If not stirred, the mixture will be soupy. Cover and place in the refrigerator for at least 6 hours, or overnight.
3. Serve with sliced bananas, toasted coconut flakes and cacao nibs/shaved chocolate. Would also be great with a dollop of coconut whipped cream!

Nutritional info (per serving): 175 calories; 7.7 g fat; 24.5 g carbohydrate; 4.7 g protein

www.ingramcontent.com/pod-product-compliance
Lightning Source LLC
Chambersburg PA
CBHW041527220426
43670CB00003B/50